THE GOSPEL ACCORDING TO

Rev. Walt "Baby" Love

Inspirations and Meditations from the Gospel Radio Legend

જે

WALT "BABY" LOVE

A Touchstone Faith / Howard Book
Published by Simon & Schuster
New York London Toronto Sydney

This book is a memoir. It relies on my memory and reflects my present recollections of my experiences over a period of years. Conversations and other events have been re-created to evoke the substance of what was said and what occurred, but are not intended to be an exact representation.

TOUCHSTONE FAITH and HOWARD BOOKS
A Division of Simon & Schuster, Inc.
1230 Avenue of the Americas
New York, NY 10020

Copyright © 2007 by Walter Shaw

First Touchstone Faith hardcover edition February 2007

TOUCHSTONE FAITH and colophon are trademarks of Simon & Schuster, Inc.

For information regarding special discounts for bulk purchases, please contact Simon & Schuster Special Sales at 1-800-456-6798 or business@simonandschuster.com.

Designed by Jamie Kerner-Scott

Manufactured in the United States of America

10 9 8 7 6 5 4 3 2 1

Library of Congress Cataloging-in-Publication Data
Love, Walt.
    The Gospel according to Rev. Walt "Baby" Love : inspirations and meditations from the Gospel radio legend / Walt "Baby" Love.—1st Touchstone Faith hardcover ed.
      p. cm.
    "A Touchstone Faith book."
    1. Christian life—Meditations. I. Title.
    BV4501.3.L687   2007   242—dc22   2006051139

ISBN-13: 978-0-7432-9165-1
ISBN-10:   0-7432-9165-4

This book is dedicated to the faithful and powerful women of God who helped raise me: my great-grandmother Susie Davis; my mother, Dorothy Barnes; my grandmother Grace Bridges; my great-grandmother Ethel Rings; and my grandmother Mittie Shaw.

CONTENTS

ONE   *From Playing It to Preaching It*   *1*

TWO   *Believe It and Receive It*   *22*

THREE   *Prepare Yourself for God's Blessings*   *42*

FOUR   *God's Got Your Back!*   *62*

FIVE   *Without God's Love, We Have No Love at All!*   *81*

SIX   *Living in His Light*   *102*

SEVEN   *Stand Up for Jesus*   *122*

EIGHT   *Know the Power of God's Forgiveness*   *144*

NINE   *Fear for the Faithful*   *163*

TEN   *Sharing God's Blessings*   *183*

     Acknowledgments   *207*

THE GOSPEL ACCORDING TO

Rev. Walt "Baby" Love

ONE

From Playing It to Preaching It

GOSPEL OF LOVE:
Know that God has a plan for you!

In all your ways acknowledge him, and he will make
your paths straight.

—PROVERBS 3:6

My first hint of God's true plan for me came from a bona
fide prophet—Prophet L. K. Johnson, to be precise. He
is pastor of my wife's childhood church, the First House of
Prayer on Chicago's South Side, and one day he pulled me
aside after his church service and said, "Baby Love, you know
you are going to preach, don't you?"

I laughed at that and told him I didn't think so.

"You've got it and you don't even know you have it," he said
with a soft chuckle.

I've got what?

"You have a call on your life from God and he will show
you the path in time," Prophet Johnson said.

I smiled politely at the elderly minister. My wife and I love and respect him, but at the time—more than a decade ago—I felt this prophet didn't know what he was talking about.

You see, I already had my own secret plan that I thought would serve my faith in the best way possible. I was then working on the launch of my own syndicated gospel music radio show. My goal was to reach millions of faithful listeners around the world. But I did not know that God had his own plan for me. His goal was to reach deep into my soul and draw me closer to him than I had ever been before.

My path began in the hardscrabble backwoods of the Appalachian foothills in western Pennsylvania, just outside Pittsburgh. My parents split up when I was a toddler and, though they later got back together, I had a nomadic childhood. After my father and mother separated, my mother, Dorothy, went to New Kensington, Pennsylvania, to study, train, and eventually work as a nurse's assistant. She left me to be raised, quite happily, in shifts shared mostly by two sets of loving great-grandparents, as well as my grandmothers and other extended family. By the time my parents got back together and restarted their family with my brother, my great-grandparents refused to give me up, which was just fine with me.

The majority of my childhood years were spent in the care of my mother's paternal grandparents, Susie and Walker Davis. They lived in company housing for the employees of the Pittsburgh Plate Glass Company in Creighton. I stayed with them during the school months and then for several weeks each summer, I'd go twenty miles across the Allegheny River, where my mother's grandmother Ethel and her husband Jim Rings had a turkey farm outside New Kensington in Plum Township.

My two sets of elderly caretakers instilled in me a nose-to-the-grindstone sense of purpose, focus, and self-reliance that helped me to do well as a student and even better as an athlete. They saw to it that everything I did was built upon a foundation of faith in God and a belief in his plans for my life. Good Christians are formed in many ways. One way is through a Christian education. I didn't really get a formal Christian education as a child, but I think I got a very good Christian education just by the way we lived and honored God at all times. Not that I was a Goody Two-shoes. I was a normal kid, a high school jock with my share of fights and girlfriends. But compared to most young guys, I was a clean-cut Christian boy. I didn't run with the rough crowd. My guardians would have none of that. I can remember them saying many times, "Lay down with dogs and you'll get up with fleas!"

I was a rural black child raised among the rough and tough white sons of coal miners and factory workers. There were no safe routes home, no easy ways out, and turning the other cheek was not an option in my neck of the woods. My guardians were strong in faith, in principles, and in pure grit. They taught me to stand up against bullies and racial taunters. I kept fighting until no one messed with me anymore. That has been a pattern for my life. I've never tried to be what others wanted me to be, and I've never shied away from facing life's challenges, trials, and tribulations.

God expects us to learn from experience. It is God's truth for us as human beings. We can't make it without him, as it says in 2 Corinthians 5:7: "Walk by faith, and not by sight."

After graduating from high school, I enlisted in the U.S. Army for Personnel Admin. School and after, true to my nature, I signed on for the most challenging assignment I could qualify for: paratrooper school. Walking by faith is one thing. Jumping out of a perfectly good airplane at just 10,000 feet is another! That is truly a *leap* of faith! I definitely put my trust in God also by beginning my military service during the Vietnam War. It was a time when many men my age were doing everything they could to avoid military duty. Yet I became a paratrooper in the famed 82nd Airborne Division. I did a tour in Southeast Asia during the Vietnam War, most of it in Thailand where we maintained a base to support operations in the region. And I survived, thanks to God's good graces.

Trusting in the Lord

In Proverbs 3:5–6, we're told: "Trust in the LORD with all your heart and lean not on your own understanding; in all our ways acknowledge him, and he will make your paths straight." I grew up under the care of men and women who always encouraged me to make my own way in the world while trusting in God's guidance. I lived among rock-solid Christians, and I never felt inclined to be anything else. Christians do need to be around other Christians so we can help keep each other strong. Yet, like most folks, I often would get so focused on pursuing career and personal goals that I'd forget that God might have his own path picked out for me.

The challenges, pressures, and distractions of everyday life sometimes force us to adopt a narrow focus. We put on blinders that block out all of the other resources available to us. But we have to fight that and work to remember that we should never trust our own ideas and views to the exclusion of all others. We must not become so self-reliant and self-determined that we become self-centered. Our egos can mess up what God has planned for us. We can't tune him out, not on his heavenly radio dial.

When I returned to the States, I was assigned to Gannon University's ROTC department as a military instructor in Erie, Pennsylvania. I carried out my day duties and then instead of partying or relaxing at night, I worked a second shift as a civilian.

With permission of my commanding officer, I moonlighted as a part-time disc jockey at a pair of local radio stations in Erie, Pennsylvania. Two of my ROTC students worked at the stations as disc jockeys and they got me interested in broadcasting. Through them, I got to know WWGO's vice president and general manager. When his jazz show host had to have surgery, he asked me to fill in, since he knew I was a jazz enthusiast. I ended up doing the jazz show whenever his regular guy was sick or on vacation. And so a broadcaster was born. But I wasn't a typical, edgy deejay. From the start, I always kept a Bible near the microphone stand. I didn't preach to anyone and I didn't wear my faith on my sleeve, but it still intimidated some. I just kept in mind the message from Proverbs 3:1–3:

> *"My Son, do not forget my teaching, but keep my commands in your heart, for they will prolong your life many years and bring you prosperity. Let love and faithfulness never leave you; bind them around your neck, write them on the tablet of your heart. Then you will win favor and a good name in the sight of God and man."*

I'd been taught to trust in the Lord with all of my heart, even when I didn't understand what was going on in my life.

My great-grandmother instilled in me that God would always make my path straight. It all comes down to trusting his plan for *your* life. But before you can trust God, you have to be willing to acknowledge him in every aspect of your day-to-day existence. Being faithful isn't a day job. Nor is it a night job. It's a way of living 24/7. You have to live your belief that God is whom he says he is and that he can and will do what he says he can and is able to do. As Jesus said in Mark 5:36, "Just believe." You've got to know that you know that you know that you know. When you truly know something like the existence of God in your life it is because you've been living with it. That faith has become a part of you and you've become a part of it. When you know something for sure in that way, it is because you *believe* it! You've got to believe that God is God and he's God all by himself. So even though I was a full-time soldier and a part-time deejay back then, my *real* job was to "just believe" and to worship God in every action. When we just do that, the Holy Spirit takes care of the rest.

Let's pause here for a brief commercial on behalf of the Holy Spirit. Some don't believe in the ministry of the Holy Spirit because they never mention him or consider him. It's my contention that the spirit has been put on the back burner for too long. The entire concept of the Holy Trinity is even denied by some Christians. I believe those folks are suffering from a condition known as the "false self." They want to think of themselves in positive terms as Christians, but they've closed the doors to God in certain areas. People who claim to be "good but not religious" are known by theologians as "nominal Christians." If they read the living word of God, the Holy Spirit will make them want to change their ways. Revelation demands response. God wants us to love him. And God's wisdom is supplied to us through the empowerment of the Holy Spirit through his word. And I was well taken care of in that regard, as you will see.

On the Air

I played "beautiful music" at WWYN and Top 40 tunes at WWGO. I'd been raised by educated and well-read folks who stressed diction so I had a natural "radio voice" with no discernible accent. Many listeners had no idea of my racial or regional background. Early in my career, I was the first black person to work on the air for several stations. I enjoyed broadcasting and the unique environment in which I spent hours each evening talking "intimately" to thousands of people I'd never seen. For someone who grew up talking to God every day, it seemed like a natural thing.

After leaving the military in 1968, I moved to Houston and took my first full-time radio job with station KYOK. Two years later, I became the first black broadcaster for Houston's Top 40 powerhouse station KILT, and the first for the Lin Broadcasting chain that owned it. This too was a nomadic sort of life. I worked my way up to bigger stations with larger audiences, breaking racial barriers at some, slamming against them at others. As a disciplined military and rural boy, I encountered additional obstacles. At KILT, I was playing Top 40, which was a combination of all types of music. Throughout the industry, radio deejays and their supervisors often seemed to emulate the hedonistic lifestyles of the recording stars whose careers they promoted. In my view, most record companies encouraged that and supported it. I refused to partake, and as a result I was something of an outsider with broadcasting insiders. Yet I was popular with listeners and with station managers who knew they could rely on me to show up sober and on time with a professional approach to my work. Still, I had to beg, plead, and scrape to get into management. After stops in Houston; Detroit; Windsor, Canada; and New York, I became operations manager at famed WVON-AM and what is now WGCI-FM in Chicago. While there, I had some memorable clashes with a dictatorial station manager. He tended to issue edicts about dress codes, facial hair, and assigned parking spaces that I refused to go along with. He fired me four times but rehired me three times!

Throughout most of my early years in the broadcasting and music industry, I bought into the perception that success depended more on who you *knew* than on who you *were.* That was a worldly view, to be sure, but it was widely held in the broadcasting business. I played along to a degree, but I stayed true to my Christian beliefs. My operating plan was to keep improving my broadcasting skills and to promote myself so that my name was always on the lips and in the minds of the executive "players" in the big markets. The radio business is a take-no-prisoners environment. Those who want to make it big have to pursue their ambitions in a big way, otherwise they can expect no mercy from the marketplace.

Yet for all of my desire to build a successful career doing what I loved—communicating with my listeners—I found that I was not comfortable with the self-promotion and self-aggrandizing that seemed to be required to gain prominence in my chosen field. Early on, my faith left me feeling lost on the traditional path to broadcasting success. But fortunately, God had his own plan for me!

My faith has always been my strength. My great-grandmother, Susie Davis, taught me as a child to always acknowledge God as the Creator of the heavens and the earth. He made us in his own image. Our Creator is awesome in his power and in his love for his creations. As I progressed in my career in those early days, I realized that my discomfort with the self-promotion and cutthroat competition of radio broadcasting was due to the fact that it conflicted with my Christian values and principles. That was a good sign because God knows; that is what those guideposts are for. They keep us on course just like those annoying bumpy lane reflectors on the highway. When you stray out of your designated lane, your tires hit those raised reflectors and it gets uncomfortably bumpy until you steer back on course. That's what happened to me.

Let me share something with you that will help make a dynamic change in your life if you'll just grab it, hold on to it, and live by it. It's the scripture that my father in the ministry, Prophet L. K. Johnson, built his ministry upon. I learned about it from my wife, Sonya, who grew up in his church, the First House of Prayer at Marquette and Cottage Grove on Chicago's South Side.

The scripture that serves as a foundation for Prophet Johnson's legendary church is Proverbs 3:5–6: Trust in the LORD with all your heart and lean not on your understanding; in all your ways acknowledge him, and he will make your paths straight.

My grandma never quoted me that scripture. But she certainly gave me the practical application of it, beginning with the admonition to always "acknowledge God, first and foremost" in my life. If I did that, she told me, he would direct my path.

Like you, I've been through some tough times. During most of my trials and tribulations in my younger years, I had my mother, Dorothy, and her mother, my grandma Grace, to talk me through and guide me along. When I was in my thirties and my mother went home to the Lord, it left a huge void in my life and in my spirit. We had spent years apart early in my childhood, but we grew closer as the years progressed. In many ways, because she was so young and full of fun, my mother was more like a big sister to me. As we both grew older, I realized that it had taken great strength and faith for her to leave me to be raised by others. But she felt it was best for me at that stage. She was the epitome of strength, courage, and faith in God.

My mother suffered from the incessant pain of lupus for many years after I left home to embark upon my military and broadcasting careers. After my mother's death, my grandmother Grace stepped up. I can still hear her comforting, assuring words: "Well, Butch [my childhood nickname], I guess me and Granddad will be your earthly mother and father for now. It looks like he has given us the job. But don't worry, honey. God will be your mother and your father. He's always there for us to call on him."

Leaps of Faith

Little did I know of the challenges that were awaiting me. They would test my faith and even threaten my life. I didn't play it safe, by most measures. Nor did I play by anyone else's rules. I became successful by making what most would have considered very risky moves. Yet I considered them true "leaps of faith" because I made them knowing that God would always be there for me.

I left management in Chicago and returned to hosting shows at top stations in New York and Los Angeles. After I became the urban radio and music editor at *Radio & Records* newspaper based in Los Angeles in 1982, the next year I developed a syndicated rhythm and blues show, *The Countdown with Walt "Baby" Love* that became the longest-running syndicated R&B show in radio and a six-time winner of *Billboard* magazine's award for best in that category. I wanted to build on the success of *The Countdown* by syndicating a similar show for gospel music lovers, a market that I considered to be greatly underserved. I realized that I could not do what I wanted to do while working for someone else, so I made a leap of faith. I left the giant syndication company where I had a lucrative contract and I launched my own business in 1995. This was before radio's consolidation binge, so leaving a major syndication company was a big risk because I was giving up a guaranteed income to strike out on my own. I started writing, producing, hosting, and syndicating *Gospel Traxx* to highlight the best in traditional and contemporary gospel music. I host and produce the show. My wife Sonya picks the music and helps set up interviews for the show. Within a short time, the show was carried on about 175 radio stations nationwide as well as fifteen countries around the world.

To create *Gospel Traxx,* I walked away from a relatively secure—and security is always very relative in the broadcasting business—position in one of the largest and most powerful syndication networks. I had to break away in order to do what my heart told me that I needed to do. I created my own syndicated radio company. God blessed me in showing me that path and then guiding me down it. He opened the door to not one but two nationally and internationally syndicated radio programs that allowed me to present his music and his message to millions of listeners around the globe.

It was a dream come true. I was using my training and talents to do what I loved to do. I was reaching people in remote corners of the world. The material rewards flowed to me. And best of all I got to play music that I love. Gospel music has always inspired me, lifted me up, and encouraged me to reflect on the word of God. My wife, Sonya, gave me a great gift when she introduced me to one of her favorite gospel songs, entitled "He That Believeth," recorded by the Chicago Mass Choir. The very first time she played that song for me, the lyrics ministered to me. At that point, I had just started the *Gospel Traxx* syndicated show. I was playing the music and working with it every day. But when I heard "He That Believeth," its message awakened me so that I listened with not only my mind, but my heart and soul, too.

That is the gift of gospel music. It connects us to God in a special way. This particular song reminded me that I had to let go and acknowledge that God is in control of my life. Christians know that, but we sometimes forget to live it. So Sonya's song was a gift to me, just as all gospel music is a gift to those who believe in God the Father, God the Son, and God the Holy Spirit.

You know, of course, what came with my initial success. I can only describe it as a restlessness of spirit, an *uneasy* feeling.

It is true that with any entrepreneurial venture, the burden of survival is always upon the entrepreneur. I was a black man who'd struck out on his own in a white man's world, so my challenges were multiplied. Still, that was not the true source of my restlessness. After all, I had not expected it to be easy. By that point, I'd even fought off kidney cancer so I'd survived serious challenges mentally and physically. Yet now, something was attacking me at an even deeper level—*my spirit.*

Solomon tells us that we must acknowledge God "in all your ways know him." This means staying in tune with him in every aspect of our lives. When we try to duck God's influence, we feel lost until we let him back into our lives. Only then do we feel fulfilled and back on track. When we let God back into our lives, we feel nothing can stop us! We have no limits! But when we cut him out, we feel like I was feeling—empty and confused.

My restlessness of spirit got so bad one day while I was driving on a Los Angeles freeway that I had to pull the car off to the side. Like a modern-day Saul on the road to Damascus, I felt this flash of anguish. I threw my hands up and cried out, "Lord, what is it you want from me? Why don't I feel fulfilled? You've healed my body and spared my life. I have achieved beyond anything I could have dreamed. Why am I not at peace?"

I wish I could tell you that the clouds parted and a shimmering ray of light beamed down upon me. But this was Los Angeles, after all. There are no clouds most of the time. Still, the sun did seem to glow a little brighter and in my head, I heard a voice that said: "I want you to serve me."

As sure as I was alive, I knew it was God's voice.

Prophet Johnson was the first person I called. I told the

Chicago minister that his prophecy had come true. God had called me to tell me that playing his gospel music was not enough. He wanted me to preach his Word as well. Matthew 22:14 says: "For many are invited, but few are chosen."

Prophet Johnson did not shy from basking in the moment. He reminded me once again of his saying that I was "a preacher without a pulpit." I'd always made a joke of his coaxing. I'd denied that God had a plan for me that went beyond celebrating his music through praise and worship with millions of listeners around the world. I thought that was enough. I thought it was my small contribution. But God didn't want a small contribution from me. He wanted something more.

Truth be told, I was a more than a little frightened of the preacher's role. Sure, I was a public figure who spoke to millions of listeners, but I did my broadcasting out of sight, in the security of a booth where it was just me and the sound engineers and a production assistant or two. Preachers are out there facing their flocks, standing at the pulpit exposed and vulnerable. I'd heard how people sniped at men and women called to the ministry. Their faith and dedication was always being measured and called into question. I had preferred to serve God in my own, quiet way, from the safety of my pew. I didn't want anyone questioning the depth of my faith and dedication to Jesus Christ.

God, however, had his own plan. Scripture tells us: "To whom much is given, much is required." I wasn't thinking clearly. I was doing what I wanted to do and not what God would have me do. Prophet Johnson had tapped into that. "I told you, Baby Love!" he said. "And now you finally know it and feel it."

He repeated what had been a constant refrain in our encounters: "I always told you that you've got it and you didn't know you had it. But now you do!"

It was true. I didn't know what it was that Prophet Johnson saw in me. I certainly didn't see it in myself. I had once asked him what it was that he saw.

"The anointing," he said. "You've got the anointing of God in and on your life. God has given you a gift."

I'd put him off at the time, out of fear or ignorance or just an unwillingness to reflect that deeply upon my faith. I was focused on building a career and providing security for myself and my family. I considered myself a devoted Christian and, by the standards of most people in my industry, I lived my faith. I'd loved gospel music all my life. I'd even played it on the air for my secular rhythm and blues show, breaking format and risking the wrath of my supervisors. I'd considered that to be a statement of my Christian faith and I'd dared anyone to challenge me for praising Jesus' name on the air.

I had not stopped to consider that the only reason I'd gotten away with my little acts of Christian defiance was because God had a plan for me. He had given me favor with my audience and my bosses. God's favor is always more important than man's perceived power. Prophet Johnson had tried to get that through my skull.

"You're going to play God's music and then you're going to preach his Word."

For a long time, I shrugged off Prophet Johnson's words without really listening to what he was trying to tell me. It struck me that day when I pulled off the freeway that he was not making a suggestion or merely trying to provoke my thoughts. He was delivering a message from above. God's spirit reached down and tapped me on the head that day, telling me to listen with my heart and soul. Things have not been the same since then. God made his move on me! And as a result, I've found a peace that I'd never known before. Now, I am serving him at a higher level than I'd ever dreamed possible.

Bible Study

I responded to God's call initially by telling my pastor, Reverend Cecil "Chip" Murray at the First A.M.E. Church in Los Angeles about my interest in the ministry. He helped me apply and win acceptance into a five-year ministry school at the Fifth Episcopal District of the African Methodist Episcopal Church in Los Angeles. It was a very good program, but in my second year, I decided to go a step further. It had occurred to me that with all of the work I was doing to become a minister, I might as well do it for college credit. I had no idea how to accomplish that until God assigned me a seat next to a messenger. I was thirsting for a deeper understanding and I thought I could find it by attending seminary school. God will help you and guide you if you ask him to. I'm not shy about asking. After all, scripture says, "You do not have because you do not ask God" (James 4:2). I prayed for additional guidance in my training for the ministry. I got on my knees and asked God for guidance. I was digging in my Bible just reading and the Spirit lead me to Isaiah 42:16, which says:

"I will lead the blind by ways they have not known, along unfamiliar paths. I will guide them; I will turn the darkness into light before them

and make the rough places smooth. These are the things I will do; I will not forsake them."

When looking for direction we have to be alert and receptive to God's leads. God uses people to get things done and to help others even when they're not expecting it. I'd failed to recognize Prophet Johnson's message from God, but eventually it came through loud and clear.

In my prayers for guidance, I read the Old Testament's book of Isaiah and found this: Whether you turn to the right or to the left, your ears will hear a voice behind you, saying, "This is the way; walk in it" (Isaiah 30:21).

The Prophet Isaiah is considered to be the greatest of all the prophets. His were the first writings of all the prophets'. Isaiah was a spokesman for God, particularly on the topic of sinful living and God's impending judgment. The people of Isaiah's time didn't listen to him or his message urging them to return to God and away from false idols such as material possessions, wealth, or celebrity. I've learned to pay better attention as I've matured in my faith. Sometimes we make the mistake of thinking that if God wants to deliver a message to us, it must come in the form of a lightning bolt or carved as commandments on stone tablets. In my case, it started with a simple question from a gentleman who was a fellow traveler, physically and spiritually. I was reading the Bible on an airplane flight when the passenger next to me asked if I was a pastor. I told him no, but that I was feeling a call to the ministry and trying to learn more.

"Have you ever thought about going to the seminary?" he asked.

It was one of those divine life-changing moments. God had

primed and prepared me for the journey, and then he put me on a flight to theological enlightenment by seating me next to Dr. Donald Hagner, who is the George Eldon Ladd Professor of New Testament in the School of Theology at the Fuller Theological Seminary in Pasadena. God looked down at one of his flock who was searching for a way to become a minister and put him in a seat next to a renowned expert in research, writing, and teaching the New Testament. I may be thickheaded at times, but it was hard to miss this message.

But just in case I wasn't tuning in, God turned up the volume. When I introduced myself to Dr. Hagner, he set me back in my seat with his response: "You're Walt Love from the radio show? My students are always quoting the things you say on your shows and asking me if you know what you are talking about. And I've got to say, every time they've questioned what you've said, I've told them that you were correct!"

Dr. Hagner was freaking me out! He scared me with that. I never dreamed that theological students would be running to their professors with the things I said on my show, but I'm sure glad that I passed the test! You know, doubts creep into the mind of every good Christian from time to time, but then when something like this occurs, there is just no denying the presence of God in your life and in the world. The Fuller Theological Seminary is one of the world's greatest schools for religious and spiritual study. I was a college dropout with only a few night courses to my credit. I might never have even applied to a school of Fuller's reputation, but Dr. Hagner opened the door and invited me in.

"I can put you in touch with the right people who will help you with the admissions process," he said.

In the beginning my wife thought I was taking on too much and that I should reconsider going back to school with all my career responsibilities and church duties and family duties. But she later became supportive.

As it turns out, Fuller has a program very much designed for people like me. They accepted me as a probationary student in their master's degree program. To stay in the program, I had to maintain certain academic standards. It took me four and a half years of night classes and many long, long nights of work because I stayed in the AME program too. In June 2005, I graduated with a master's degree of arts in theology. I intend to pursue my doctorate in ministry at Fuller.

I truly believe that my meeting Dr. Hagner was a divine encounter. None of us can know how, when, where, or why God will make a move on our lives by sending a messenger or working a miracle. What we do know is this: He is able to do whatever he chooses, whenever he chooses, however he chooses. Jesus was given the power to heal when he started his public ministry. He healed the sick, restored sight to the blind, got the lame to walk, and even raised Lazarus from the dead. When Jesus was on his way to Jerusalem to be crucified for our sins and redeem us to his Father, he came across a blind beggar. This story always inspires me because it shows how persistence in seeking Jesus pays off. The beggar was sitting by the road when a crowd came along and he asked what was happening.

"Jesus of Nazareth is passing by," he was told.

The blind beggar seized the moment by calling out: "Jesus, Son of David, have mercy on me!"

When people tried to quiet him down, he cried out all the louder.

"Son of David, have mercy on me!"

Jesus heard him and asked to talk to him. When he came near, Jesus asked him: "What do you want me to do for you?"

"Lord, I want to see," the blind man said.

Jesus responded: "Receive your sight; your faith has healed you."

Immediately he received his sight and followed Jesus, praising God. When all the people saw it, they also praised God, according to Luke 18:35–43.

Faith is a healing force. We need to remember that when we are hurting physically, psychologically, and spiritually. When we feel blinded or blindsided, we have only to ask God to help us see. And then, we have but to open our eyes to his blessings and to accept his plan for us. There are substantial benefits for those who trust in God's plan. A primary benefit is that you build upon your relationship with God Almighty. Then he starts giving you his personal protection. You belong to him!

Hold on. Hold on. That doesn't mean you are home free or trouble free for the rest of your natural existence. In fact, you'd better be ready for the devil to come knocking all the harder on your door. The dark angel will come for you just like he did for Job. And God just might let the devil beat you up a little, but he will ultimately protect you because he has work for you to do. The devil only has the latitude that God allows him. The same is true for you and me. Acknowledge God. Trust God with your life. God has delivered me from death's door, physically and spiritually, more than once. I survived because I trusted in his path for me. Just like in the song "I've Got a Testimony," when I look back over my life and I think things over, I can truly say that I've been blessed. It's not just about *doing* in this world, it is about *being*. Jesus was the epitome of *being* while also *doing* in this world. That is why we all need to be more Christlike in our daily lives. Acknowledge God and trust in the Lord with all of your heart. Praise God no matter what happens. Keep praising his name. Keep giving him glory.

Since my own days of struggling, I've adopted as my mantra this from Jeremiah 29:11–13:

> *"For I know the plans I have for you," declares the LORD, "plans to prosper you and not to harm you, plans to give you hope and a future. Then you will call upon me and come and pray to me and I will listen to you. You will seek me and find me when you seek me with all your heart."*

Trust me. God's got a plan for your life too!

ॐ

> *"Fear not, for I have redeemed you; I have summoned you by name; you are mine. When you pass through the waters, I will be with you; and when you pass through the rivers, they will not sweep over you. When you walk through the fire, you will not be burned; the flames will not set you ablaze. For I am the LORD, your God, the Holy One of Israel, your Savior."*
> —ISAIAH 43:1–3

ॐ

TWO

Believe It and Receive It

GOSPEL OF LOVE:
Believe in the power of God's promises

"If you believe, you will receive whatever you ask for
in prayer."
—MATTHEW 21:22

I was about eleven or twelve years old when Walker Davis—my great-grandfather—died of kidney cancer. His death was scary in a couple of ways. It's devastating as a child to lose someone you love, honor, and respect. Granddad Davis was the best. He would bounce me on his right knee and pretend it was a pony ride. He'd allow me to watch him shoot his hunting shotgun, and he'd always let me help him fix things even when Grandmother Susie would say, "That boy is in the way, Mr. Davis."

He'd reply, "Ah, Susie, let him be. I have to teach him how to take care of you if I'm not here to do it."

Then he would laugh and give me a big hug.

It was scary to lose him and his strong, loving presence. The other frightening aspect of his death was that without him, we feared we would lose our home. We lived in "PPG housing" in Creighton, Pennsylvania. The rental houses were owned by my great-grandfather's employer, the Pittsburgh Plate Glass Company. Our house wasn't fancy, but it was comfortable. It was a little row house made of wood. We had cold water, but no hot. If you wanted hot water, you had to heat it up in a pot on the kitchen stove. If you needed a lot of hot water, you put another one on the potbelly stove in the living room. My grandmother didn't care for that at all.

The house had two bedrooms but no bathrooms. Like everyone else in our humble neighborhood, we had an outhouse. It could be a very cold walk on winter mornings. But usually your misery had company. There were sixteen dwellings in our little neighborhood; five black families and eleven white families, and everyone got along. In that part of western Pennsylvania, back in the day, families looked out for one another and individuals did the same. Of course, there was a second set of nicer row houses down the road about a mile. (Someone is always going to have it better, right?) Only white families lived there. Naturally, they had hot and cold running water as well as indoor bathrooms with a tub. That was the deluxe section as far as we were concerned, and though we never talked about it outside the family, we secretly hoped that one day we might get to move on up to that neighborhood.

Yet when my great-grandfather died, my great-grandmother and I feared we might be required to leave the company-owned housing altogether. Our security was threatened. Grandmother Susie was very worried because she was way up in age and afraid that she would not be able to get a job to pay for another place while raising me, too. My mother and father, who had their own struggles, were not giving her any financial assistance.

Perfect Storms

Now, I realize how difficult it must have been. I don't know how my great-grandmother did it, really, but she handled all of these challenges without venting her fears or frustrations. Still, I was old enough to pick up on her concerns about our housing. It was a period that is still very vivid in my memory because I felt so helpless and vulnerable. When I reflect back on that time now, I can still feel the fear that ran through me. It's something that I tap into now and then because it reminds me of the power of God's promises. We all feel fearful, vulnerable, and exposed from time to time. Sometimes it is an emotional thing; at others, a physical thing. Memories of the fears that I felt as a boy back in Pennsylvania always are stirred when I read certain passages in the Bible, particularly the vivid descriptions in the Gospel of Mark dealing with Jesus and the disciples when they were caught out on a boat during a squall (Mark 4:35–41).

Who better to create the "perfect storm" than the son of God? If it wasn't perfect, it was close enough to scare the heck out of the disciples on board. They were scared down to their sandals, and they couldn't believe that Jesus was asleep in the stern. When the waves started coming up over the bow and into the boat, they woke him:

"Teacher, don't you care if we drown?"

Jesus got up, stretched, and then commanded the wind and waves to "Quiet! Be still!"

The waters went calm as the squall dissipated in an instant.

Then Jesus calmly turned to his disciples and said: "Why were you so afraid? Do you still have no faith?"

I think the modern nonbiblical term that might apply to the disciples' reaction here would be "freaked out." They totally freaked out.

"Who is this? Even the wind and the waves obey him!" they said of Jesus.

This little boat trip was really a lesson in faith: *"If you believe, you will receive whatever you ask for in prayer."*

In their defense, the disciples didn't have the perspective that we have today. They were living the gospel in real time. Jesus was flesh and blood to them so it was more difficult for them to imagine him as the all-powerful son of God. They saw the dirt under his fingernails. They watched him stumble as he walked. He was a man to them, so it was difficult for them to conceive that this truly was the son of God who'd been sleeping in their boat during the squall. They should be forgiven for not getting it right away. After all, they were worried about going overboard. The Sea of Galilee is not really a sea. It's a big lake that today measures seven miles wide and twelve and a half miles long. But it's not a kiddie pool. The Sea of Galilee is known for sudden storms that turn it into a big surly whirlpool tub. It is located 680 feet below sea level and surrounded by towering hills. When the winds come a-blowing across its waters, they stir up hellacious storms that seem to come up from the darkest recesses of the earth.

It is true that most of the disciples weren't exactly landlubbers. At least four of the apostles—Peter/Simon, James, John, and Andrew—were experienced fishermen from Capernaum on the Sea of Galilee. They'd spent a good part of their lives on the water. Yet those aboard this trip got panicky because the squall threatened to wash them all overboard. And they were stunned that Jesus was taking a catnap at the height of the storm. That's the great thing about being the Son of God. While others might be losing their cool, turning green from seasickness, and fearing for their lives, you can catch up on your sleep! In truth, Jesus slept with God's own comforter. He had faith that his Father would watch out for him! And he couldn't understand why his disciples did not have the same empowering faith.

Storms come to our earthly lives in many forms. We all experience physical storms like the squall on the Sea of Galilee or the killer hurricanes that have tormented the southeastern United States in recent years. Then there are the emotional storms that strike us when we lose a loved one or experience tragedy, illness, or financial crises. These psychic storms cause anxiety and stress that is every bit as debilitating as being deep-sixed in the Sea of Galilee. You know the feeling. I know the feeling. We *all* know the feeling. Every last drop of blood in your body seems to drain out the soles of your feet, doesn't it? You get light-headed, woozy, disoriented, and panicky.

And then those nagging, paralyzing questions start popping up in your mind and just keep on coming: *What am I going to do? How will I ever get through this? Why is this happening to me? Why can't I see a way out of this?*

It always feels like the most complex, mind-numbing quandary the world has ever thrown at your feet. Yet, as is so often the case, the solution begins with the simple realization that there are only two options to be considered.

OPTION ONE: *You can take all the worry into your heart and assume that Jesus no longer cares about you or what happens to you.*

OPTION TWO: *You can express your love of God, confess your need for his help and forgiveness, and then trust that if you believe, you can achieve.*

Jesus said: "I shall never leave thee, nor forsake thee."

My advice is to heed his words. When panic, anxiety, and stress drain the blood from your veins and send your mind reeling, express your love for him, confess your need for his help, and then trust in his divine love. Don't underestimate God's power for love and forgiveness. You might be tempted to scoff at the reaction of the disciples who feared for their lives as the squall hit their boat and Jesus slept. Yet we have had the Bible and the word of the Son of God here on earth for more than twenty centuries and we still underestimate him. We still doubt him. We still wonder if Jesus is asleep at the wheel and unmindful of our need for his help!

The disciples knew Jesus as a man. They didn't have the benefit of twenty centuries of writings and teachings and miracles. At the time of the storm on the Sea of Galilee, Jesus was just beginning to reveal his powers. Word was just beginning to get out and it wasn't like the disciples had the nightly news or the internet to spread it. Word of mouth was the only "mass media" of that day. In fact, some of the disciples themselves— Matthew, Mark, Luke, and John—would become the world's most famous communicators through their writings of Jesus and his time on earth. They chronicled his exploits, his miracles, his death, and his resurrection so that we might believe and receive his grace.

Casting Demons

They also recorded Jesus' power over evil, so that we could understand that no force can stand up to his almighty goodness. When the squall subsided at the command of Jesus, the disciples continued their journey across the Sea of Galilee to "the other side." According to Mark 5:1–20, they arrived at a village known as Gerasenes near modern-day Israel's border with Jordan.

As Jesus and the disciples, who were probably still soaked from the squall, climbed out of their boat, they were approached by a crazed man who'd come running from the tombs where he lived among the dead. He was thought to be possessed by evil spirits. He was so wild that he'd been kept in chains and irons, but he'd broken free of them. He was so strong that no one could control or subdue him. Yet he was also tormented. We're told that he would cry out all night from his hiding places in the tombs and surrounding hills. He also would cut himself, apparently trying to release the evil within him.

Jesus recognized the demons that possessed this stranger and commanded, "Come out of this man, you evil spirit!"

The crazed man, in turn, recognized Jesus as "Son of the Most High God" and asked him not to torture him.

Jesus calmly asked the man to tell him his name.

"My name is Legion," he replied, "for we are many."

Now, it should be noted that in those days a Roman legion

consisted of six thousand men and was regarded as one of the most powerful forces of the period. So, this one poor man was obviously not in control of himself. In his writings on this incident, Mark reports that the demons within this tormented man asked Jesus to "send us among the pigs; allow us to go into them."

Jesus gave the demons permission to leave the man and to enter a herd of pigs feeding nearby. There are nearly two thousand of the swine, and when the demons entered them the entire herd rushed down a steep bank, fell into the lake, and drowned! Naturally, news of this event spread quickly through the region—even without CNN, Fox News, or internet bloggers. When people who'd heard the story came out to see Jesus, his disciples, and the crazy man, they were amazed to find Legion now acting and talking like a normal person.

Oddly, this made people afraid. Maybe it was just human nature, but they feared a man who could order demons to depart. Some of the people pleaded with Jesus to leave the region for fear of reprisals against him.

The disciples convinced Jesus to get back in the boat. Legion asked to go with them, but Jesus wanted him to spread the word. He instructed him to tell his family what had happened and to speak of the mercy that he'd been shown. You see, Jesus knew he had to get the word out so that more would believe that he was the Son of God and be willing to receive his grace just as Legion had. For those who enjoy symbolism, the name of this man is fascinating. Jesus undoubtedly wanted to make a point that many, many people—whole legions of us—are possessed of sins and tormented by the evil forces of Satan. Yet God and his Son are quite capable of forgiving all of us and exorcising our demons so that we can receive them into our hearts as Christians.

Satan's evil is nothing to mess with. The story of Legion is thought to be the most powerful and violent exorcism in the gospel of Mark. Those who lived on the Jordan side of the Sea of Galilee were Gentiles in Jesus' day, so he was also sending a message that his healing love and grace were available to all who were willing to believe and receive it. The same holds true today, centuries later, of course. All we have to do is ask him into our hearts and believe, and, as the Bible says, "confess with our mouths" that Jesus Christ is Lord.

Just Believe

So Jesus is back in the boat for a return trip. If you know your Bible readings, you are aware that Jesus made a total of six crossings during this time period. He was working the area, getting the word out, preaching and performing miracles more often in order to reach out to more and more people. His Sea of Galilee tour with the disciples was very successful at accomplishing those goals. By the time their boat returned to the other side of the lake, there was a large crowd waiting for them. One of those along the shore was a synagogue ruler named Jairus who was truly a believer already. When Jesus and the disciples came ashore, Jairus fell to the ground at Jesus' feet and implored him for help.

His daughter was dying, he said, "Please come and put your hands on her so that she will be healed and live."

Obviously, this man believed, so Jesus went with him to reward him for his faith. The crowd followed them, eager to witness a miracle. As they approached the home of Jairus, they were met by some men who informed them that his daughter had just died.

"Why bother the teacher anymore?" they asked, referring to Jesus.

But Jesus insisted on seeing the deceased child.

"Don't be afraid," he told Jairus, "just believe."

With those simple but powerful words, Jesus entered the house, ordering everyone else to stay outside, except for his disciples (or apostles) Peter and James, and his brother John. Inside the house, they found people weeping and wailing in grief. Jesus put a stop to their mourning by announcing that there was no reason for it. "The child is not dead but asleep," he said.

Some laughed at him. Others were probably angry or resentful. Jesus asked that everyone but the girl's mother and father leave the house to him and his disciples. There was something about his manner that made them obey even if they doubted him. Once the others had left, Jesus escorted the parents to the bedside of the daughter. He then took the child's hand and said, "Talitha koum," which in Aramaic means "Little girl, I say to you, get up!"

Immediately, the child rose from the bed and got to her feet as if awakening from a deep sleep. Jesus then ordered her parents to feed her to help restore her strength. Naturally, word of this miracle spread throughout the region and, as we know, it was recorded in the writings of the apostles and became one of the great stories on which our Christian faith is built. Jairus believed and so Jesus allowed him to receive his blessings and grace by healing his daughter.

Salvation Awaits

One of the most important promises in the Bible is the promise that if we believe in Jesus Christ as our savior we will be saved and we will have everlasting life. Belief is paramount for us to have faith. So believing that God exists and that he is the creator of all things is a must. There are no ifs, ands, or buts if we are to stand on the promises found in the Holy Bible. Once we've got that down, we can begin building upon it and deepening our faith in God and what his love means to us as his creation.

Belief and faith go together, because if you don't first believe, you can't have faith. The New Revised Standard Version (NRSV) translation of the same scripture from Hebrews 11:1 says: "Now faith is the assurance of things hoped for, the conviction of things not seen." The NIV translation gives us another interpretation: "Now faith is being sure of what we hope for and certain of what we do not see." The next verse tells us something very important about God's character and his relationship to his creations—that's you and me: "This is what the ancients were commended for."

God commended people in the Old Testament era because of their faith and trust in him. Even when facing calamities that seemed overwhelming and never ending, they held to their faith and believed God would protect and deliver them. We are the seeds—the descendants—of Abraham, which means we are heirs to his blessings and the promises made in the Bible are passed on to us. That is something to keep in mind and in your heart. We must persevere at all cost. Hebrews 10:23 always gives me hope in Jesus: "Let us hold unswervingly to the hope we profess, for he who promised is faithful." Sometimes you may get weary and feel like throwing in the towel, but I'm here to give you hope. My life is a testimony to the power of believing in God and serving him. When I was a boy, I sometimes couldn't contain myself. I'd talk about something exciting I'd learned in Bible studies at Sunday school and I'd often get teased as a result. I got in a fight once with my buddy Booker, who liked to yank my chain whenever I talked about Jesus. Booker seemed to question whether there was room enough for him and Jesus in my circle of friends outside of church. He jumped all over me when he heard me tell some kids that God had created the heavens and the earth.

"Who said so?" Booker demanded. "Prove it!"

Booker's grandmother, Mrs. McIntyre, was my great-grandmother's close friend. They went to church together and Booker was in my Sunday school class. He'd had the same lessons. But he didn't want to hear me talking about God on the playground. He was one of those guys who thought Jesus belonged in church. The playground was his turf. Well, Booker and I got into it big-time that day. He ticked me off so bad that day I started to cry and then I pushed him in the chest and told him to shut his mouth. I guess at that point I was a passive-aggressive Christian soldier. It wasn't exactly what Jesus would have done. Some other kids broke up our little spat, but Booker continued to taunt me at every opportunity. "Prove it," was his byword in matters of faith. I would learn that there are many like Booker out in the secular world who would challenge my faith.

In Hebrews 10:35–39, we are urged not to "shrink back" or back down when we're being persecuted or facing extreme pressure from nonbelievers. We must hold on to our Christian beliefs and our faith. We owe God that for sending his son Jesus down among us to suffer for our sins. That same passage in Hebrews advises us to not throw away our confidence in God's existence, because we will be richly rewarded. "You need to persevere so that when you have done the will of God, you will receive what he has promised." We are reminded that in just a very little while, "He who is coming will come and will not delay. But my righteous one will live by faith. And if he shrinks back, I will not be pleased with him." In other words, don't get on God's bad side!

Again and again in the Bible, we're told that we've got to be-lieve to receive. John 6:47–48 says: "Very truly, I tell you, who-ever believes has eternal life. I am the bread of life." That's a quote from Jesus taken from the New Revised Standard Ver-sion of the Bible. That's why he said on so many occasions to people who sought him out "Just believe."

There are a number of scriptures that tell us about the mir-acles and wonders that Jesus performed. I love reading those stories because I know in my heart they are true. I know the Bible is God's breathed word for us to live by and for us to gain encouragement and strength from as believers. The story of Lazarus is only found in the Gospel of John in chapter 11. I encourage you to read the story when you need inspiration and reinforcement because it offers so many lessons on the power of faith. Lazarus, who was a longtime friend of Jesus, fell terri-bly ill. His sisters Mary and Martha sent word to Jesus: "Lord, the one you love is sick." Jesus got the message, but he did not drop what he was doing and come. Instead, he stayed away for two days, telling those worried about Lazarus: "This sickness will not end in death. No, it is for God's glory so that God's

Son may be glorified through it." Later, he reassures them: "Our friend Lazarus has fallen asleep; but I am going there to wake him up."

Lazarus died while Jesus was away. The disciples didn't know. They thought he was really resting. But then Jesus finally told them it was time to go to him, noting, "Lazarus is dead, and for your sake I am glad I was not there, so that you may believe." Jesus and his entourage finally show up in Bethany to find Lazarus has been entombed for four days. His sister Martha was not a happy camper, telling Jesus that if he'd come earlier Lazarus might not have died. But she hastens to add that she believes that God will do whatever his Son requests.

Jesus calmly tells her: "Your brother will rise again."

Martha figures that Jesus is talking about the end of the world and the final reckoning sometime down the road, but Jesus has his own timetable for Lazarus.

"I am the resurrection and the life. He who believes in me will live, even though he dies; and whoever lives and believes in me will never die," Jesus said.

He then asks Martha if she believes.

"Yes, Lord," she told him, "I believe that you are the Christ, the Son of God, who was to come into the world."

Jesus then asked to go to Lazarus' tomb. Scripture tells us that:

> *Jesus, once more deeply moved, came to the tomb. It was a cave with a stone laid across the entrance.*
>
> *"Take away the stone," he said. "But, Lord," said Martha, the sister of the dead man, "by this time there is a bad odor, for he has been there four days."*

Then Jesus said, "Did I not tell you that if you believed, you would see the glory of God?"

Don't just read this, feel it in your heart and in your soul.

"Did I not tell you that if you believed, you would see the glory of God?"

Jesus broke down and wept at the tomb of his friend. He cried for Lazarus and for the sorrow of his sisters Mary and Martha. Then, Jesus delivered on his promises. He called Lazarus out of the tomb and when Lazarus came out, Jesus instructed his friends and family to "Take off the grave clothes and let him go."

That is the power of faith. That is why when Jesus sends you a message, it's for real and you should believe it! "For God so loved the world that he gave his one and only Son, that whoever believes in him shall not perish but have eternal life" (John 3:16).

Power of Faith

"Believe and you will receive!" As with so many things in my life, I learned that first from my great-grandmother, and only later did I realize she was passing on a lesson from scriptures. Like the disciples in that rocking boat, lessons came to me when all I could think about was bailing and holding on. My great-grandmother taught me to look for strength in the scriptures in such challenging times, and her wisdom has guided me ever since. She often quoted this scripture and it has served as a pillar of strength in my life. Hebrews 11:1 says, "Now faith is being sure of what we hope for and certain of what we do not see." Another translation says this: "Now faith is the substance of things hoped for, the evidence of things not seen."

Jesus is my hope and always has been, even when I wasn't walking with him as closely as I should have been. Stronger now, my faith continues to drive me to this day. We should always remember what the Holy Bible tells us in Romans 10:17: "Consequently, faith comes from hearing the message, and the message is heard through the word of Christ." My contemporary translation says it this way: "Faith comes by hearing and hearing the word of God when it is preached."

It's important to understand that we must continually hear God's word proclaimed. Yes, we can read it daily in our private Bible studies, but it is important to hear it preached too.

The Bible is the road map to life. It's the all-time manual for us to read and live by if we hope to serve the Lord. All my life, the preached word has inspired me and encouraged me to not only keep on going but to have even more faith and trust in the power of God. When the crisis over my great-grandfather's death arose, I didn't want my great-grandmother to have to clean some white lady's house to support me. At her age she deserved to be supported and treated with respect. I was only about twelve, but I wanted to step up like a man and get a job to do that. It distressed me to hear her crying and praying for God's help and guidance when I thought she should be relying on me instead. I'd hug her and wipe her tears and tell her that I would "fix" our financial woes. She forced a smile and said, "Baby, you aren't old enough to get a job."

I told her I could shine shoes, wash cars, or do chores to earn some money so I could give it to her.

"I know you'd take care of me, but God will take care of us. We have to have faith."

The power of her faith gave me comfort. My great-grandmother often broke into song when she talked to me about our Christian faith. She did this when things were good and when things were bad, too. In this situation, she sang her favorite gospel song, a spiritual entitled "Near the Cross." Its lyrics offer hope in a "precious fountain . . . free to all a healing stream."

Like many spiritual songs, this one rises from a mood of deep despair but offers hope of everlasting life through Jesus. My great-grandmother sang it to remind herself of God's grace and the hope that lies within it. I summon up memories of her singing when I need uplifting, too, even today.

"Near the Cross" is found in most hymnals where there are predominately African American congregations. It is interesting to me that more and more mainstream Christian denominations, including the Roman Catholic churches, are embracing the favorite spirituals and gospel songs of African American worshippers. The Catholic church even has a popular hymnal called *Lead Me, Guide Me* that contains many of my favorite gospel songs. And I'm glad to share them.

My great-grandmother believed in the goodness of God and all of his creatures, and her faith proved out over time. Faith in God guided her life and it has guided mine as well. I've since learned how to "walk by faith and not by sight." The NIV translation says: "We live by faith, not by sight." We may not see it right now. But if we can just believe as Jesus told us to do, it's coming. God can do anything. The question is, Will he?

That's where faith comes in. Still, I've learned that you've got to fight for your faith or face no hope of salvation. There are those in the world who would have us reject God the Father, God the Son Jesus, and God the Holy Spirit and his commandments. Only your belief in Christ will save you and assure that God the Father will count you among the righteous.

A few weeks after my great-grandfather's funeral, the manager of the PPG plant where he'd worked contacted my great-grandmother. He told her that my great-grandfather had been a wonderful employee beloved by his coworkers.

"You don't have to worry about moving, Mrs. Davis," he told her.

My great-grandmother had confessed a need for God's help and she had then trusted that his blessings of grace and mercy would come. And they did, raining down upon us for weeks, months, and even years. I think that after all those years of praying, she had a direct line to heaven's switchboard! Yes, she was one dialed-in Christian!

Once again, the disciples in the boat with Jesus lacked perspective. They feared for their lives because they knew him in human form, with all of his frailties and flesh-and-blood vulnerabilities. It's easy for us to look back a couple thousand years or so and say the disciples foolishly underestimated the fellow asleep in the stern of their boat. But how often do we do the same thing—even with all we know today? Even with hundreds of years of Christian teachings. Even in a day and age when you can Google the Bible chapter and verse quicker than a theologian can thumb through his scholarly notes.

Weeks after great-granddad was buried, neighbor after neighbor and church member after church member stopped by with sympathies and prayers. Many of them were white folks who told stories of my great-grandfather and the kind things he had done for them. Some brought food. Some left cash on a counter without comment. My great-grandmother did get some money from her husband's pension, his insurance, and from Social Security, but we would have struggled mightily if it hadn't been for the generosity of those people, most of whom didn't have much themselves.

God's mercy came through the plant manager and numerous family and church friends. My great-grandmother told me that, and I believe it today just as I did then. God has shown himself faithful through thick and thin in my life.

In fact, it was only a year later that the plant manager moved us on up into one of the fancier row houses I mentioned earlier. You should have seen my great-grandma! She did the Holy Hallelujah dance right there in our little—and I do mean little—kitchen. She said to God, "How great Thou art!" Hallelujah! Hallelujah! Hallelujah! Oh, God, I love you. Thank you, Jesus, for allowing me to be loved by you but also by this Christian earthly family I was born into.

Here's the kicker. Our old housing was integrated with whites and a few black families, but we'd always been told that the better neighborhood was just for whites. But God is color-blind and so is his power. He sent beams of love and compassion through the plant manager and with his spirit moved, he allowed us to become the first black family to move into the much nicer housing. Our presence allowed more black PPG employees to upgrade over the years, so the pebble in the pond rippled for a long time after that.

Good All the Time

African American Christians are fond of the phrase *God is good all the time; and all the time God is good!* Scripture tells us in Romans

8:28 that "all things work together for good." The (NIV) translation says: "And we know that in all things God works for the good of those who love him, who have been called according to his purpose." I know my great-grandmother and my great-grandfather were "called according to his purpose." One of his purposes was for them to raise me in their Christian home and pass along their faith and values so that I might become a person called by God just as they were. My great-grandmother used to tell me that I was going to become a preacher, a minister of God. I always said it would never happen and when she asked me why not I'd say, "Because people don't give men of God the respect they deserve and they don't make enough money!"

But in fact, her words were prophetic, God bless her. She spoke it into existence and now I'm humbled that the Holy God I serve not only called me, but he has chosen me as one of his servants. I'm an ordained elder and preaching the word of God just like she said I would. Praise God!

ॐ

And whatever you ask for in prayer, having faith and [really]
believing, you will receive.
—MATTHEW 21:22

ॐ

THREE

Prepare Yourself for God's Blessings

GOSPEL OF LOVE:

Put yourself in position to receive God's blessings

Then He said to her, "Daughter, your faith has
healed you. Go in peace."

—LUKE 8:48

Today when someone juggles several jobs at the same time,
it is known as "multitasking." We called it "survival."
Most of the men and the women I knew growing up worked
two or three or four jobs. African Americans didn't usually
draw the top dollar on a payroll, so those who aspired to better
their lives—or at least to pay the bills—found the strength to
go on and work another job when many other folks punched
out and went home. My mother, Dorothy, was a prime example. I had to live with other relatives because of the hours she
put into a variety of full- and part-time jobs. She worked two
days a week cleaning a wealthy city official's home while also
doing nightly custodial work at Myers Furniture Store in New

Kensington and working a regular shift at North Hills Passavant Hospital in Pittsburgh.

Many days my mother would say how tired she was, but she took responsibility for her own welfare. She didn't ask for charity. She looked for any way she could to earn money, and she always thanked God for the opportunities that she found. Sometimes during my visits with her, I'd go out on her jobs with her and help her, and it was always exhausting just trying to keep up with her sweeping, dusting, vacuuming, and cleaning. She earned her own way and she prepared herself for God's grace, believe me.

Having faith in God and preparing yourself for God's blessings is imperative. How many times have we all heard it: *God helps those who help themselves!* My family was chock-full of Christians who believed deeply in God, but they also understood that he does not want us to spend our lives in church pews praying for heavenly blessings to rain down upon us. He wants us out in the world aggressively preparing ourselves in the same way that the wise farmer puts seeds down and fertilizes the soil so that when the rain and sunshine come, the crops will rise and flourish.

Growing up in poverty, I saw many people—within my family and outside it—living inspiring, godly lives in spite of the hardships and challenges. Many of them were strong women, including my mother, grandmother, great-grandmother, and another member of my extended family who has been a huge blessing, my Aunt Jean. A retired registered nurse now in her eighties, she allowed me to experience God's love through her attention and affection. In her younger days, Aunt Jean worked in the mill at Pittsburgh Plate Glass along with many other family members. But she believed that God wanted her to serve others, so she prepared herself for his blessing by quitting her job in the mill and taking an entry-level position at a local hospital. It was a bold move to step outside the security of the factory back then. But she felt a calling. As a strong Christian, she put her faith in the Lord and her talents to work.

Preparing the Ground

A man reaps what he sows. The one who sows to please his sinful nature, from that nature will reap destruction; the one who sows to please the Spirit, from the Spirit will reap eternal life. Let us not become weary in doing good, for at the proper time we will reap a harvest if we do not give up. Therefore, as we have opportunity, let us do good to all people, especially to those who belong to the family of believers.

Aunt Jean trained and became an operating room technician, but sometimes she also worked alongside my mother and her sister, Miss Ora, cleaning at Myers Furniture Store. Later, Aunt Jean used the money she'd earned to enroll at Allegheny General Hospital School of Nursing, where she earned her nursing degree and passed the state boards—when she was fifty years old! It was a source of inspiration to us all that Aunt Jean was still putting herself in position for God's blessing even as her youngest son, Lenny, was working on his undergraduate degree at Carnegie Mellon and her oldest, Pete, was earning his Ph.D. at Kent State University.

We like to think that we have control over our lives and where we are going with them. But in truth, we have no control over what God hands down to us. We can only play the hand we are dealt, pray for his blessings, and trust in his goodness. I have learned the hard way that my plans are not always in God's own daily planner. Often, he has other ideas for me. Eventually, this is made clear to all of us, either through enlightenment or by rude awakenings. We can plan and scheme all we want, but God has the last word on the course our lives take.

Over the years, I've done my best to prepare myself to receive God's blessing by acknowledging him in every aspect of my life and living by his commandments. Like most, I've strayed from God's path. But believe me, I'm not crazy! When you love God, it only takes one slap upside the head from the Holy Spirit before you get back on course. When God decides to allow his blessings to manifest themselves in your life, you've got to be ready as a child of God. You can't be a couch potato and expect God to pick you up and move you to the head of the line. If you have nothing to offer society, then God has nothing to work with. You need to get motivated, educated, polished, and presentable so that when your number is called by the heavenly Father, you are ready to step up and answer the call.

As a boy and into my teens, I dreamed of being a professional football player because of my success as an athlete. But I had my pragmatic side too, because I had a plan for a career after football—as a social worker! My radio broadcast dreams were sparked by the great early rock-and-roll deejays, both black and white, who took to the airwaves in the 1950s and 1960s and enlivened the nights of teenagers across the country. I held on to that dream during my nearly seven-year military career. I prepared myself for God's blessing in that regard by reading everything I could find on the music industry, its entertainers, composers, producers, promoters, and broadcasters. I stayed in touch with my childhood buddy, Jeff, who was working at WWRL in New York. He had introduced me to Chuck Leonard, the first and only African American on-air talent at the Top 40 powerhouse WABC at that time. They sent me tapes of their broadcasts to play for my army buddies and I listened to them continuously, training myself while entertaining myself too. As I listened to their tapes, I thought again and again *What a way to make a living!*

I got in a little extra preparation as master of ceremonies and member of a five-man band and singing group that performed in enlisted men's clubs for our fellow soldiers. I also worked part-time at a couple of radio stations while still in the military back in the United States. During all of this time, I prayed for guidance and read the Bible to keep myself on track. So when God was ready to bless my broadcasting career, I was prepared to accept it and run with it!

The Roman philosopher Seneca said, "Luck is what happens when preparation meets opportunity." That is true in all aspects of life, whether it is your relationships, your career, or your spiritual development. In relationships, a guy can never hope to attract the girl of his dreams until he becomes the man of *her* dreams. In building a career, you have to learn the basics before you can become a leader and pacesetter. And in our spiritual development, we have to prepare ourselves for God's blessings by becoming worthy servants. "Land that drinks in the rain often falling on it and that produces a crop useful to those for whom it is farmed receives the blessing of God. But land that produces thorns and thistles is worthless and is in danger of being cursed. In the end it will be burned" (Hebrews 6:7–8).

That verse goes on to tell us that "God is not unjust; he will not forget your work and the love you have shown him . . ." and notes that "We do not want you to become lazy, but to imitate those who through faith and patience inherit what has been promised."

As Christians, we understand that the Holy Bible is our road map to consult when we feel lost and need direction. By reading and reflecting on his teachings, we can prepare ourselves for God's blessings and for the lives he maps out. Yet it is also important to put ourselves in position for those blessings. It is good to pray for help from above, but the Lord is more likely to bless someone who is also striving to make things happen down here on earth.

This is one of the messages I see in Matthew 9:18–26. There an ailing woman sought Jesus in a crowd and reached out and touched the edge of his cloak. We're told that she had been "bleeding for twelve years" and she'd decided that "if I only touch his cloak, I will be healed."

Now, many in the crowd were taken aback by this woman's bold move. For one thing, she was considered "impure" because of her bleeding in those days, and it was actually against the law for Jesus to have contact with her. This desperate woman had faith in his healing power, but she knew she had to put herself in position to receive Jesus' blessing so she defied the laws of the day and reached out in the crowds around her to touch his cloak.

As soon as she did this, Jesus realized that healing power had gone out from him. He stopped and said, "Who touched my clothes?"

His disciples were puzzled because there were all sorts of people crowding around him, yet Jesus had picked up on one individual. Still, Jesus kept looking around to see who had done it. Finally, the fearful woman revealed herself by kneeling at his feet. Trembling with fear, she told of her illness and of what she had done in hopes of tapping into his healing graces.

People in the crowd expected that Jesus would rebuke the impure woman for daring to touch him, but instead he announced to everyone that she had his blessing.

"Daughter," he said, "your faith has healed you. Go in peace and be freed of your suffering!"

Wouldn't we all like to hear those words from the Son of God? *Go in peace and be freed of your suffering!* In saying this to the ailing woman, Jesus was delivering the message to us all that if we believe as strongly as she did, if we put ourselves in position, he will offer his blessings and his healing power! Keep in mind that this particular incident was a big deal back in the day. People then lacked our basic knowledge of the human body; they considered her bleeding to be a curse. She was a social outcast, an untouchable in many ways. She was not supposed to be out in public, let alone touch anyone—especially someone of the stature of Jesus. Yet Jesus welcomed her effort to help herself by coming to him. In healing her, he tells us that his grace and love extend to all people willing to ask for it and accept it.

Do you believe in the healing power of faith in Jesus? Obviously that woman who tracked down Jesus in the crowd believed in it. And she was rewarded for her conviction. Good Christians know that there is no limit to God's power, and in recent years even scientists have acknowledged the healing power of faith. Dr. Harold Koenig, an MD, is head of Duke University's Center for Spirituality, Theology and Health, which is among the first research facilities in the world to study how religious faith affects believers' physical and emotional health. Now, God's word in the Bible is enough to convince me that faith heals both the spirit and the mind, but if science wants to do its own homework, that's okay with me. In fact, the researchers at Dr. Koenig's center have made a number of interesting "scientific" discoveries that support what many Christians have long believed.

Dr. Koenig has spent more than two decades studying the impact of faith on believers' physical and emotional well-being. Among his scientific findings:

- *Those of faith who've gone through physical illness experience* significantly *better health outcomes than people who are less religious.*

- *Those who go to religious services on a regular basis have stronger immune systems and lower stress than those who don't.*

- *Strong religious beliefs seem to protect the elderly from cardiovascular disease and cancer.*

- *People of faith recover from hip fractures and open-heart surgeries better than nonbelieving patients.*

In his book, *The Healing Power of Faith,* Dr. Koenig documents the fact that people suffering from alcoholism, anxiety, drug addiction, depression, polio, heart disease, and myriad other medical challenges have recovered their health and gone on to productive lives through spiritual means.

Faith in Action

When I think about the mystery of life and the mysteries of God, I'm just blown away at the thought of his almighty power and love for us as his creations. But I believe that God is more inclined to help those willing to help themselves. The book of James tells us in chapter 2, verse 26 that as the body without the spirit is dead, so "faith without deeds is dead."

James is saying that true faith leads to good works. If you have faith, you live it and express it in your attitudes and actions just as God ordains it. A bit earlier in James (2:22), Abraham's faith is described: "You see, that his faith and his actions were working together, and his faith was made complete by what he did." I've heard it said that our actions express our faith just as our bodies are the physical manifestation of our spirits. People know we are "alive and kicking" by our physical presence, and we express our faith, true Christian faith, by our actions on this earth. Now, it is possible to have faith without doing good works just as the spirit exists long after your body is gone. That's exactly what James is referring to in 2:18 when he says: "But someone will say, 'You have faith; I have deeds.' Show me your faith without deeds, and I will show you my faith by what I do."

These passages tell us that faith and works are peas in a pod. Jesus was no stick in the mud when it came to putting his faith into action. He could have stayed up on a mountaintop somewhere and prayed during his time on earth, but instead, he went out into the world and walked the talk! He fed the hungry. He clothed beggars. He visited and healed the sick. He was both a man of faith and a man of action. And Jesus didn't tell the apostles to express their faith in him by praying all day. He tells them in Mark 16:15,16: "Go into all the world, and preach the Good News to everyone every where." And again, James offers this message in 2:24: "You see that a person is justified by what he does and not by faith alone." I recommend that all Christians read the entire book of James. It is only five short chapters, but the blessings contained in them are many. You will find guidance there that will help you to recognize opportunities to open yourself up to God's blessings. When I was in the military wondering what to do with my life when I got out, my mother said, "Son, Mama wants you to reach for the stars. You can do it. But if you don't get it, God will still give you the moon."

Before I was old enough or smart enough to read the Bible on my own, my great-grandmother, Susie, often reminded me that God wants his children to live their faith and to not only pray for his blessings but to prepare for them too. My nickname as a child was Butch, but she preferred calling me Walter. She'd say, "Walter, you have to do good things for other people so you'll be ready for God's blessings. You have to be kind to folks and help them because God wants us to love one another."

She didn't just tell me that. She lived it and served as an example to me. Every day I got to see the love of Jesus through my great-grandmother. I saw her work hard to take care of our family while also reaching out to neighbors and church members experiencing the storms of life. People going through hard times were drawn to her because of her loving kindness, her anointing, and her wisdom. My great-grandmother was a woman of powerful faith who put it into action every day of her life.

After my great-grandfather's death, we lived on what remained of his PPG pension and the Social Security checks. It was not much. We were used to the "not much" lifestyle. I know my grandmother prayed for God's blessing, and her prayers were answered. But it's interesting that the answer to her prayers came as a response to her Christian acts. When my great-grandfather was alive, and even after he passed, my great-grandmother shared whatever she had with our friends and neighbors in need. Her generosity was an unconscious expression of her faith. And when those same people sensed that we were in need, they responded.

I can still envision my great-grandmother sitting in our living room or at the kitchen table listening to the radio. There would be a knock on the door and a neighbor man or woman would come by. White or black, they walked into our humble home respectfully, almost as if entering a chapel. It was a godly place, to be sure. And these people would chat with my great-grandmother a while before coming to the reason for the visit. A neighbor woman would come by or a neighbor man and they would talk about something nice my grandfather or grandmother had done and they would reach in their pockets and say, "Miss Davis, I just brought a few dollars to help you out." It might be twenty or even fifty dollars. And that would pay the bills for the month.

Or sometimes they would never address the purpose. They would just get up, say good-bye, and walk out after leaving something on the table. The point is that God would send somebody to do something kind for us, and often they would express that it was in response to kind actions that my great-grandparents had done for them.

As a boy, I observed the faithful strivings of my family members and unconsciously I adopted their self-determination and work ethic. I put my faith in God, but I also kept my nose to the grindstone so I'd be in position for opportunities he presented to me. Some people can't understand why anyone would jump out of a perfectly good airplane at ten thousand feet, but when I was in the military that was my role as a paratrooper, *plus I got fifty-five dollars a month extra in "jump pay"!* Most of my fellow paratroopers thought that was enough work for one person, but I usually had an after-hours job working somewhere off the base.

Often, I'd get on with a custodial company because their crews worked the late shifts, when I had free time. Most people thought it was beneath them to do such dirty and menial work, so those jobs were plentiful. But I grew up around custodial workers and I was glad for the opportunity to work as hard as those who had raised me. I'd change out of my work uniform fatigues into work civilian clothes, get on the bus to Fayetteville, North Carolina, after 6:00 P.M. to do hard labor until midnight sweeping and buffing floors and cleaning bathrooms.

Some of the guys in the barracks would razz me, saying, "Hey, Shaw, you leave after work every evening and we don't see you until late at night. You got a woman or something in town? You partying? Where do you go?"

At first I'd tell them it was none of their business, but finally I tired of the game and told them straight up. Still they wouldn't believe it.

"You've got another job on top of what we do all day here?"

Those who did believe would laugh at me or mock me for being such a grinder. Only a few expressed any admiration. Now and then I'd hear something like "Man, whatever it is you are working for, you are sure dedicated to getting it."

Everyone in my company and certainly those in my platoon knew I was a Christian. But I was a Christian soldier who would kick butt if someone tried to bully or take advantage of me because of my faith. More than once I had to ask God's forgiveness for straightening out someone who'd mistaken my Christian beliefs as a sign of weakness. It was a rugged environment, and I was not as mature in my application of my faith as I might have been. I just felt that God was probably too busy to strike down my tormentors, so I did it myself.

Occasionally, someone would mock me and my faith to provoke me: "Why don't you just pray for what you want and let God take care of it?"

Christians hear that question a lot. It's an interesting question. If you believe in the power of prayer, why not just pray for all you need? Even Jesus had his moments in which he asked for God's help and for relief from earthly burdens. In Matthew 11:28, Jesus says,

> "Come to me, all you who are weary and burdened, and I will give you rest. Take my yoke upon you and learn from me, for I am gentle and humble in heart, and you will find rest for your souls. For my yoke is easy and my burden is light."

Jesus is saying that he is there for those who need him most, the weary and burdened. He is gentle and *humble of heart* and willing to provide rest for the souls of those who most need him. But I believe that we can pray for God's assistance even as we take steps to help ourselves. That way, God sees that we are willing to take responsibility for our own lives too. Whatever your burden—whether it is a health issue, a money problem, relationship challenges—you should always put yourself in position to receive his blessings. Don't cower in a corner, hide under the covers, or spend your days holding pity parties. Instead, open your heart to God's grace by getting as close to him as possible.

You might be having troubles at home or on the job or in both aspects of your life. It happens! It can also happen that you are having difficulty being Christlike in your everyday actions. God knows we all have challenges in that department! Don't get down on yourself. Don't give up on your faith. Welcome Jesus and the love, peace, and joy he brings to the table—or tabernacle. Reach out to him so that your needs will be met by his goodness.

The Christian life doesn't come with a ten-year-guarantee. And churches have yet to join electronics and appliance stores by offering extended warranty "deals" at the checkout counter. So there are no guarantees that living a good Christian life will relieve you of any and all challenges, burdens, and earthly torment. Some of the most devout people I know have led tormented lives, and how many blatant sinners do you know who appear to lead charmed existences?

God has a plan though he may not be sharing it with you today, tomorrow, or ever! Because we may never understand God's plan for our lives. But he will put an arm out and help you walk with him when he sees you taking steps in the right direction. I do believe that God will provide all our needs because scripture says that he knows our needs. But I also believe that you've got to put yourself in position to receive God's blessings. Praying for miracles is a way to exercise your faith. It's commendable to seek his help and guidance. But my advice to you is to do your praying while you are working toward your own solutions.

Sometimes even good Christians mistakenly think that they can't go to God. But, trust me, you can. We all can. He is listening for your footsteps, waiting for you to approach him, hoping that you will make an effort that he can reward. We are God's children. God waits like a good parent who knows she can't walk for her child. The child must learn to walk without assistance. A good parent stands back and encourages and cheers but does not move the child's legs for him. We should never allow our fears to keep us from taking those first steps in our approach to God. I felt his call to the ministry, but the Lord wasn't going to go to the Fuller Theological Seminary in Pasadena and register me for classes. There were times when I prayed to God for help with all the class work I had to do, but in his wisdom, he allowed me the pleasure of writing all those scholarly papers on my own.

One of the hardest things about pursuing a degree at the Fuller Theological Seminary while also running my own syndicated radio business was the drive home after class each night. Often, I wouldn't get out of there until 10 P.M. or later. It was a long drive home. My brain was on overload.

To lift myself up, I'd put in the Byron Cage gospel song "The Presence of the Lord," written and produced by Kurt Carr. It has a very fast and upbeat tempo, which was just what I needed after a long day and longer night. It is such an uplifting song that it always raised my spirits. It got me so pumped up I'd have to watch myself. I tended to put the pedal to the metal when listening to that song.

Gospel music often has that effect on me. It fills me with

joy and revitalizes my enthusiasm for my walk with God. The lyrics of "The Presence of the Lord" encourage us to feel the Lord in the atmosphere and in our hearts, and to feel blessed in the moment. Hearing that song always makes me feel more positive and optimistic. It reminds me to let God's spirit work within me and it reminds me to take nothing, especially my Christian faith, for granted, because when you put that faith in action, it becomes a powerful force.

Jesus was not angry when the ailing woman approached him in the crowd and touched his cloak. Of course, he knew who'd done it, but he stopped and made a lesson of it so that others would learn the power of faith put into action. Genuine faith involves action. Faith that isn't put into action is not faith at all. Do you need an example? Perhaps one of the best modern-day exhibitions of faith put into action is the remarkable organization Habitat for Humanity, which is a Christian ministry that builds homes on a foundation of faith. As someone who knows what it is like to live in poor folks' housing, I can't help but think God must look down on this organization and smile his most beatific smile. In its dedication to eliminate inadequate housing and homelessness worldwide, Habitat for Humanity strives to create affordable and decent shelters as a "matter of conscience and action." There's the A-word again! Just saying it out loud gets your heart pumping a little faster: *Action!*

If you are looking to put your faith into action but don't know how to do it exactly, I suggest you learn by first acting to help others. You will be surprised at the benefits and the spiritual boost you get by volunteering for Habitat for Humanity or a similar Christian organization. They welcome volunteers and supporters from all backgrounds, and with the destructive hurricanes and tsunamis of recent years, they have more than enough work for everyone. There is no mistaking the spiritual roots of this organization. They present each recipient of their faith-based actions with not only a new home but a new Bible as well! The folks at Habitat for Humanity will tell you that their group, which operates around the globe, is driven by the desire to "give tangible expression to the love of God through the work of eliminating poverty housing."

What I love about Habitat's ministry is the way they follow the teachings of Jesus Christ by loving and caring for others. Habitat gives people the opportunity to put their faith and love into action. Interestingly, Habitat officials say that they also put to use two other key concepts: "economics of Jesus" and the "theology of the hammer." I like these because they are real-life examples of walking the talk—in this case, the talk is the lessons of the Bible. The economics of Jesus is based on a simple formula. When you and I reach out to help others, God joins in and multiplies the power of our efforts! For proof of this, just consider that Habitat's volunteers and its "sweat equity" home owners have built safe and secure homes for more than 200,000 around the world. You can't look at that figure without knowing that God's own power and love were at work alongside everyone else.

Habitat's "theology of the hammer" concept, developed by founder Millard Fuller, says that while Christians of all faiths may disagree on some things, they agree that building homes for God's needy people—for no profit—is a statement of faith. Habitat for Humanity is the embodiment of faith in action. Whether building a home for a needy family or trying to build a life for yourself, you have to step up, get off your knees and onto your feet, and take those steps of faith. Get in position to receive his blessings!

Consider this: Maybe you haven't gotten what you wanted from God because you haven't shown him how badly you want it! Doors open only when you take action by knocking or turning the key. To open the doors to your dreams, you must put faith into action. Get off your knees, out of bed and off the couch, and let God know that you are doing your share so that he can do his. If you think just praying is enough, it is not. Nor is fretting and worrying. Jesus taught this in Matthew 6:27 when he says: "Who of you by worrying can add a single hour to his life?" Then down in verses 30 through 34, he really breaks it down to them.

"O you of little faith? So do not worry, saying, 'What shall we eat?' or 'What shall we drink?' or 'What shall we wear?'

"But seek first his kingdom and his righteousness, and all these things will be given to you as well. Therefore, do not worry about tomorrow, for tomorrow will worry about itself. Each day has enough trouble of its own."

We've got to keep our eyes on the prize! Our salvation through Jesus Christ is the prize. It is the reward and the zenith of our Christian walk with the Lord. When I think about self-determination and the ways of the Lord, I'm always reminded of the joke about the thickheaded believer trapped in a flood. His house is surrounded by rising floodwaters, so he climbs up on the roof. A rescuer in a boat comes by, but the believer says, "No, go ahead and pick up someone else because I can wait. God will take care of me."

Then a helicopter hovers overhead and drops a rope ladder,

but again the believer says, "No, the Lord will save me." Finally, the floodwaters rise over the top of his house, sweep him off the roof, and he drowns.

When the believer arrives at the Gates of Heaven, he finds Jesus waiting, tapping a sandaled foot.

"Why didn't you save me?" the believer asks.

"Well, I sent a boat and then a helicopter. What were you waiting for?"

Some people miss the boat—and the helicopter—over and over again. They have their eyes so tightly closed in prayer that they can't see God waiting for them to get up and open the door to his grace. My grandmother used to laugh about the people who would pray to God to send them a hundred dollars instead of asking him to help them figure out how to earn it themselves.

Have faith in God and believe that he will answer our prayers. But, more important, put yourself out there where God can see that you are ready, willing, and able to accept his assistance and guidance. The first step, of course, is to accept Jesus Christ as your Lord and your Savior. God will not force us to accept his Son Jesus. The Bible teaches us that we are "justified" by faith if we believe in Jesus Christ who died for our sins and that God raised him from the dead. Our justification comes through our being Abraham's children.

Scripture says that God counts us righteous if we believe in Jesus. Romans 3:22–23 says this:

> *This righteousness from God comes through faith in Jesus Christ to all who believe. There is no difference, for all have sinned and fall short of the glory of God, and are justified freely by his grace through the redemption that came by Christ Jesus.*

I want you to believe because I want everyone who can be saved to be saved. Believing is just part of the process of being saved. Here's the clincher that will get you where you want to go: Praise God! It's right here in Romans 10:8–10 and then verse 13. Verse 8: "The word is near you; it is in your mouth and in your heart," that is, the word of faith we are proclaiming. If you confess with your mouth, "Jesus is Lord," and believe in your heart that God raised him from the dead, you will be saved. For it is with your heart that you believe and are justified, and it is with your mouth that you confess and are saved. A little farther along verse 13 says: for "Everyone who calls on the name of the Lord will be saved."

If you believe, you are putting yourself in position to receive God's grace. Once you confess Jesus Christ is Lord, the blessings will begin because you will be saved. Glory! Hallelujah!

ॐ

Everyone who calls on the name of the Lord will be saved.

—ROMANS 10:13

ॐ

FOUR

God's Got Your Back!

GOSPEL OF LOVE:
Trust God and hold on to your faith, especially
during times of trouble

"For I am the LORD your God, who takes hold of
your right hand and says to you,
Do not fear, I will help you."
—ISAIAH 41:13

O ne of the things I've certainly learned to accept from life
is the simple and undeniable fact that *stuff happens*. And
don't we all know that the bad stuff happens when you least
expect it? Of course, Jesus was way ahead of me on this. He
tells us in the second part of John 16:33, "In this world you
will have trouble. But take heart! I have overcome the world."

Yes, take heart! There is deliverance from the world's daily
trials and tribulations. You find it in your love of Jesus, in your
faith, and in your hope. I found it as I was heading toward the
ground at more than forty miles an hour with a messed-up
parachute trailing behind like so much limp spaghetti! This fall

from the heavens—but not from grace—occurred during a paratrooper training jump at Fort Bragg in my soldiering days. It was a mass training jump involving yours truly and several thousand of my closest paratrooper pals.

Barreling bodies were all over the place that day, but stuff *happens!* Of all the descending bodies that day, there was one—mine—that was falling faster than all others. And this was not a race! As you may suspect, vivid memories of that moment are deeply etched in my mind. It was a beautiful day for jumping (though not all that great a day for falling). The sun was shining in a cloudless sky. Our entire battle group, the 505th Airborne Infantry Brigade of the 82nd Airborne Division, was pumped for the big jump. AIRBORNE . . . ALL THE WAY!

Things went smoothly in the early going. We rolled out to the staging area in our "cattle trucks," secured our equipment, and drew our chutes from the riggers. After donning our equipment, we were put in groups and assigned to aircraft. We went up in C-130 transports that day. I never liked jumping from the smaller C-119s or the C-123s. I'd already learned that seasoned jumpers preferred the big planes like the C-130s and the C-141s because they were the most stable aircraft. Of course, I only cared that they were stable up to the point when I jumped out of them.

Once the plane was in the air and en route to our drop zone, we got into position, which was no easy task given the gear and the crowd and the cramped confines of the transport aircraft. I was about fifteenth "on the stick," which is the line formed by paratroopers at the side doors that lead to nothing but open sky and unrelenting gravity. Like everyone else, I carefully went through the mandatory equipment checks and other safety procedures. Then our jumpmaster gave his commands: *"Stand up! Hoop up! Check your equipment! Sound off for equipment check!"*

Starting at the back of the aircraft the paratroopers up and down the two sticks—one line for each door of the C-130—began calling out their designated position numbers.

Next came the command to stand ready to jump: *"Stand in the door!"*

It's not quite as macho as it sounds because each paratrooper is standing like a penguin packed into a holding pen with his flock of jump mates. You've got on all this cumbersome gear, so all you can do is shuffle/waddle one or two steps at a time toward the door. No, it's not macho at all until the green light flashes and the jumpmaster yells, *"Go! Go! Go!"*

He keeps yelling as guys leap out into the blasting wind like lemmings leaping off the cliffs. This is known as "hitting the blast." Just before I reached the door, the guy in front of me stumbled or slipped and hesitated. This threw off the rhythm of the entire stick. We bumped into each other in what might have looked like a comical chain reaction except that I wasn't laughing. I was too busy trying to recover. But I got jostled and couldn't get my proper balance. As I moved forward I wasn't in a stable position for my jump. As a result, I hit the blast twisting and spinning in the wind like a kite that lost its tail.

Struggling to regain control, I recalled my training, counting off the seconds as I looked up to see if my main chute was open. That is when I realized that I had what paratroopers call a "Mae West." It's not a good thing. It happens when the suspension lines of the parachute are out of position. They run up over the top of the air-filled canopy and crimp your chute until it resembles a busty woman's bra. It's an amusing name but not an amusing situation. If you've got a Mae West in your chute, that means there is not enough air in it and you are falling much too fast for a safe landing.

This is when you have to trust in your ability to follow your training as a paratrooper. And you have to trust that the training you've received is going to work. I was taught to react to a Mae West by opening my reserve chute in a special manner so that it does not become entangled or twisted in the main chute and make it any worse. You do that by covering your reserve chute with your left hand as you pull the rip cord so that the pilot chute with the spring on it doesn't come out before you want it to. You are then supposed to feed out the reserve chute by hand so that it goes past your main chute and blossoms fully, slowing your descent to a safer speed.

As I tried to do that, I quickly realized that I had another problem—or maybe I should say that I realized I had more trouble than I could handle. When I went to pull my reserve, the pilot chute slipped out and got by me and started entangling itself in the already-twisted suspension lines. I had to do everything I could to keep that reserve from collapsing what little main chute I had left to slow my descent.

I knew that if I allowed my reserve to open completely, it would only make the situation worse by further reducing the air in my main. As fast as I was falling, I could still hear the eerie calls from my fellow troopers on the ground yelling up: "Pull your reserve! You can do it! Come on! Come on!"

But I'd already pulled it to no avail.

I will never forget thinking, *Oh help me Jesus! Help me make it!*

With only a portion of my chute collecting air, I was falling faster than I'd ever experienced, but it seemed like my mind was cranking in slow motion. I was running through my options, trying not to think about what would happen if I didn't come up with something. I did not lose faith, either in God or in myself. And I'm very grateful for that. I'm a big believer in faith and hope; it's been ingrained in my character since my childhood. There I was, an adult, a soldier in the United States Army, a grown body plummeting toward earth, but the voice in my head was a boy's voice, my own, calling upon Jesus, summoning up the faith instilled in me by my great-grandmother. Hebrews 11:6 says: "And without faith it is impossible to please God, because anyone who comes to him must believe that he exists and that he rewards those who earnestly seek him." Glory to God! Not only do I believe he exists and that he rewards those who seek Him, I also know he has all power in his hands. I'd been taught that Jesus gladly reaches out to those who have fallen. I was just hoping, on that day, that he would reach out to one who was fall-*ing*.

Scripture says: "We walk by faith and not by sight." My sight said everything was looking pretty awful, but my faith said I was going to make it. Jesus said that even if your faith is no bigger than a mustard seed, exceptional things can happen. I'd learned to believe faith and prayer serve to draw God's favor into our lives. Jesus told his disciples they could pray for anything and whatever they asked for in his name, they would receive it!

"Have faith in God," Jesus answered. "I tell you the truth, if anyone says to this mountain, 'Go, throw yourself into the sea,' and does not doubt in his heart but believes that what he says will happen, it will be done for him. Therefore I tell you, whatever you ask for in prayer, believe that you have received it, and it will be yours" (Mark 11:22–24).

I was fighting for my life, plummeting toward the ground with minimal drag from the twisted parachute. I looked down, saw nothing but ground coming at me, and called his name: "C'mon Jesus, we're going to get through this one!"

It was a dire situation, and I was feeling like King David himself as he faced his own mortality. So what better time for some of Psalm 27?

VERSE 1: *The LORD is my light and my salvation—whom shall I fear? The LORD is the stronghold of my life—of whom shall I be afraid?*

VERSE 2: *When evil men advance against me to devour my flesh, when my enemies and my foes attack me, they will stumble and fall.*

VERSE 3: *Though an army besiege me, my heart will not fear; though war break out against me, even then will I be confident.*

VERSE 4: *One thing I ask of the LORD, this is what I seek: that I may dwell in the house of the LORD all the days of my life, to gaze upon the beauty of the LORD and to seek him in his temple.*

VERSE 5: *For in the day of trouble, he will keep me safe in his dwelling; he will hide me in the shelter of his tabernacle and set me high upon a rock.*

My own day of trouble on high ended abruptly. Thanks to the wonders of gravity and the Mae West in my parachute, I came down to earth in mid-psalm. My platoon sergeant said I was doing about 45-plus miles per hour. I came in at an angle so I hit and then I rolled. It was not a textbook PLF—parachute landing fall.

I briefly did an impression of a tumbling tumbleweed and then, miraculously, I popped up on my feet like Jackie Chan doing a stunt. But it was just instinct kicking in. I was in shock. I was loopy from the hard landing. My head was spinning. My body was a bruise in progress. Two medics rushed up and made me sit down. One of them beamed a little flashlight in my eyes and made the obvious diagnosis: "He's in shock."

The shock was that they didn't have to peel my corpse off the ground with a spatula. Instead, they put me on a stretcher and transported me to the base hospital where doctors said I had a slight concussion. The good news was that I still had a brain rattling around in my skull and, miraculously, no broken bones. I learned two very important lessons on that ill-fated jump:

1. *None who believe in God are ever alone.*

2. *Do not leave a perfectly good airplane except in a perfect body position.*

Now, I definitely get the whole "God is my copilot" concept. I felt his presence all the way to the ground. I don't know what plan he has for me, but apparently, my life was not supposed to end in a puff of dust and a tangle of descending lines. I was a strong Christian before I jumped out of that plane, and I don't think surviving that fall made me any stronger. But it certainly made me more aware of his presence in my everyday life.

I've always known that God is holy and powerful. I've always known that he is the source and sustainer of life. And now I know, every second of every day, that God has my back!

When I reflect on this incident I think of this powerful gospel song sung by the Gospel Music Workshop of America Mass Choir. It is called "Your Testimony Starts with a Test" and the featured singer is Angela Spivey, who has a beautiful voice. The message of this song is that life is a test. Your testimony to God's total control of life is your witness of God seeing you through the challenges of each day, week, month, and year. It was certainly a test when I fell that great distance from the jump plane to the ground. And when I lived through it, my life became a testimony to God's continued presence in my life. I lived to jump another day. I walked away from that understanding that when you are one of God's children, the fix is in!

Christian Soldiers

It wasn't always easy being a Christian soldier, and I sure wouldn't claim to have been anyone's model for a perfect person at that point in my life—or any other. Rural Pennsylvania wasn't always a friendly place for a young black guy. The older I got, the uglier the racial taunts became. These were the sons of miners and steelworkers and factory workers, so it was a tough crowd. My great-grandmother raised me as a Christian, but she also told me, "Don't you let anybody take anything from you. If you have to fight, you fight. If you lose, you will live to fight the next day, but you have to make them understand you aren't going to take it. You may not win every time, but keep fighting until you do."

I had to walk through an old brickyard in Creighton to get

to the school playground, and when she found out that kids were threatening me there, my great-grandmother didn't advise me to run or find another route. "When you go through that brickyard, pick up some brick," she said. "Put it in your pocket and if someone comes after you, throw the brick and hit them."

It is always a struggle to live our faith and to stay on the path. But in my Bible readings I did find fellow soldiers, warriors, and heroic Christians whose own trials and tribulations, and faith, helped me through the challenging times. King David, in particular, was a mighty warrior and leader who ruled for forty years and engaged in many battles with his powerful enemies. Yet David, father of Solomon, was very much a typical man who struggled with his flaws and failings just as we all do. That is what makes him such an appealing role model for me and many others who aspire to be soldiers of Christ but face our own human challenges.

David's words in Psalm 27 are known as some of this poet-warrior's most comforting writings. It offers insight into not only his conflicting emotions, his hope and confidence that the Lord will support him, but also his powerful need for God's reassurance. Can't we all identify with that as we struggle in our daily lives to be strong of faith? David proclaims in his psalm that God is his *light*, his *salvation*, and his *stronghold*.

Conflicted Christians

Jesus is often described as "the light" or as a source of light in the Bible. In a world of constant conflict—the darkness we all face—it is comforting to think of our savior as one who provides illumination to chase away the shadows and our fears. In

the New Testament, the disciples often cast Jesus in such terms. Paul describes Jesus as living "in an unapproachable light" (I Timothy 6:16). John stays with the metaphor in his writings that note: "God is light; in him there is no darkness at all" (I John 1:5). And "If we walk in the light, as he is in the light, we have fellowship with one another, and the blood of Jesus, his Son, purifies us from all sin" (I John 1:7).

It's no wonder then, that when people described near-death experiences—such as falling to earth with a tangled parachute—they describe visions of "walking toward the light." For Christians, Jesus is the light in a world of darkness and shadows. We struggle and strive to keep his light on in our lives at all times. The darkness and the light represent the conflict of good and evil, God and Satan. And so we want to always light it up in the name of Jesus. In his Old Testament psalms, David, the conflicted poet-warrior, maintains that even faced with the darkness and evil of war with his enemies, he has no fear. Instead, David has faith illuminated by the light of God.

David's faith, my faith, your faith; give us the blessing of hope. As true believers we are never without hope. Even as I fell to earth with my parachute messed up, I had my faith and, therefore, I still had hope that I would survive. And I did! (However, based on the advice of my lawyers, I must add the following note: *Kids, don't try this at home!*)

The first six verses of Psalm 27 record David's faith in God and his hope for his own salvation, and then his confidence appears to waiver a bit beginning in verse 7 as he implores God for help. As a Christian soldier, I can identify with that and I'm sure you feel the same way. We are flawed, frail, and sometimes foolish human beings. Faith and hope are shields that we can

wield as we battle our weaknesses and the challenges that the world hurls at us out of the darkness. You develop faith and hope in God by having him in your life. Our faith and hope will see us through such battles as long as we hold on to them, but it certainly doesn't hurt to ask for God's help in the fight.

We all face conflict with our enemies, within ourselves, with the world around us. Jesus himself dealt with one conflict and confrontation after another during his public ministry on earth. Let's get real: Jesus was confronted by Satan himself, by darkness and evil spirits. God knows we all face similar challenges to those faced by his Son here on earth. Jesus said, "Don't be afraid; just believe." So we must do as Jesus did. We must ask God the Father to deliver us when we are faced with conflict and confrontation. David dialed the heavenly 911. Jesus did too. I mean if you've got the friends and family plan, what is there to stop you from putting in the call?

Jesus is the door to the Father so you can go knocking there first if that's how you want to play it. All you have to do is ask him into your life as your Lord and as your Savior. God will deliver you! You just have to trust him and believe in him. You have to believe that he will take care of you. You have to believe that he is able. You have to believe that he is God Almighty and that he is the God of healing. I was definitely holding on to that God of healing thought after I smacked the ground on the drop zone at Fort Bragg!

Like David, we are Christian soldiers who believe and have hope, but in the heat of battle our doubts and fears sometimes creep in and we need reassurance. That's why we pray and read the Bible. Part of Exodus 15:26 tells us that if you listen carefully to the voice of the Lord your God and do right in his

eyes, and if you pay attention to his commands and keep all of his decrees, you will be protected. As I discovered in my unplanned free fall as a paratrooper, sometimes God doesn't simply step in and save you. Sometimes, he rides it out with you all the way to the very end to test your faith in him. So keep that in mind. Don't give up on God. Church is not the only place he dwells. Your holy savior may be alongside you in your hospital bed, in the emergency room, in your wrecked car, in the courtroom, in the drug rehabilitation center, in the jail or prison cell. As David noted in his psalms, God is your salvation and your stronghold. God is the source and sustainer of life. We feel God's presence by becoming obedient to him. We surrender our lives to him and then our thinking begins to change.

Confidence in His Love

Know that the LORD is God. It is he who made us, and we are his; we are his people, the sheep of his pasture. Enter his gates with thanksgiving and his courts with praise; give thanks to him and praise his name. For the LORD is good and his love endures forever; his faithfulness continues through all generations (Psalm 100:3–5).

When you face conflict and challenges, you will undoubtedly experience fear and uncertainty. It is only human. But it is essential that Christians remain confident in Jesus' love. It's okay to worry, as David did in his psalm, but it is possible to remain confident in the Almighty's goodness at the same time. I didn't fully understand this myself until I reflected on my parachuting mishap. I realized that I never gave up on God. I still believed in him and his love for me. Yet that didn't stop me from trying to find a way to slow down my descent! *But* I failed. I did not find a way out of my plight, and still I survived a fall that very easily could have killed me or left me paralyzed for life!

Believing is one thing. You have to *trust* God. As a Christian, I believe I have to trust God because I really can't trust anyone else. I believe that God is the Supreme Being. If we don't believe that, we are lost. We know that good people die too. And sometimes they die too young, or tragically, but the Bible tells us it rains on the wicked as well as the righteous. Bad stuff happens to us all. But that doesn't mean we shouldn't believe. I wish Christians got special favors, but God is bigger than all of us. Life's not fair and God doesn't play favorites. So we still have two choices: to accept God as our Savior or to not accept God. It may sound easy but it is not. Life is not easy to live, and having Christian faith is a constant battle. You've got to hold on. You can't give up. If you give up, you are definitely lost. I believe God rode to the ground with me and he saw me through!

Of Whom Shall I Be Afraid

"The Lord is the stronghold of my life—of whom shall I be afraid?" writes David in the last part of his verse. King David, like me, was a military man who faced imminent danger. And I'm sure in his earlier trials, he wondered if God was going to step in and save him. I can think of one obvious scenario when that happened. It's the story that even non-Christians know:

the story of David and Goliath. It is a powerful story because God referred to David as "a man of my own heart." When all of the soldiers of Israel were afraid, the shepherd boy said, I believe in God and I am not afraid. This story resonates with all people through time because it is such a powerful story of Christian faith.

The boy David returned to his shepherding after being anointed king. He was probably uncertain of what else to do with himself as he was still just a youngster. We don't hear much about him until Saul and the Israelites go to war with their enemies the Philistines, regarded as a superior fighting force, in the Valley of Elah. There, they faced off from separate hilltops divided by the valley. Goliath, a huge warrior from Gath, challenged the Israelites by walking alone into the valley. We're told he was nearly ten feet tall, that he wore heavy armor of bronze, and carried an iron-tipped spear.

This imposing warrior, who was supposedly descended from a famous family of huge fighters, challenged the Israelites to send down a champion of their own for a winner-take-all battle. As was the custom then, Goliath said that if he won, the people of Israel would become the subjects of the Philistines, and if he lost, he and the Philistines would become the subjects of Israel. Apparently, Saul and the Israelites weren't thrilled with this offer, but I've got to say it sounds pretty appealing to me. Think of the lives that would be saved if we settled all wars in this manner!

Young David was not with the Israeli army to hear Goliath's initial challenge. He was still back home in the family pastures, taking care of his flock, singing and playing his harp, we're told. But his three older brothers were soldiers assembled on the hilltop overlooking the Valley of Elah. As it happened, Goliath's challenge caused a standoff that lasted for more than a month because no one in the Israeli army wanted to face the giant. During the standoff, David's father sent him to check on his brothers and to return home with news of how the battle was going. David was there visiting with them when Goliath appeared in the valley to issue his daily challenge. David's brothers explained to him that the towering warrior was the reason the war was at a standstill. Other Israeli soldiers chimed in, saying that if anyone did manage to survive a fight with Goliath, the rewards from King Saul would rain down upon him. They mentioned great wealth, marriage to one of the king's own daughters, and no taxes for his entire family. To a shepherd boy, this undoubtedly sounded like a pretty sweet deal, and in his youthful arrogance, David, who'd been out with his sheep a long time under some pretty challenging circumstances, figured he could handle the giant warrior. At least, that's what he told his brothers. He may have just been spouting off to appear tough to them, but other soldiers heard him and word spread quickly that there was one among them who was willing to challenge Goliath. Soon David found himself standing in front of King Saul, who wasn't impressed with what he saw. But then David boasted to him that he had protected his flock by killing both a lion and a bear with his own hands. The boy, it seems, had come to believe that God had his back! I know, because his words to the king are reported in Scriptures.

"The LORD who delivered me from the paw of the lion and the paw of the bear will deliver me from the hand of this Philistine," he tells King Saul in I Samuel 17:37.

The king bought it. He had his soldiers dress David in his own tunic, coat of armor, and bronze helmet. They also gave the boy a sword, but David quickly decided that he couldn't fight in the king's clothes or with the king's weapon. He stripped off the armor and helmet and headed down the hill with only his staff and his throwing sling. Near the bottom of the hill, he stopped at a brook and picked up five smooth stones from it, and put them in his shepherd's bag.

Now, there are military experts who will tell you that David's approach to the battle with Goliath came to serve as a model for future warfare in which smaller, swifter, more mobile, lightly armed forces were able to defeat bigger, stronger but less agile foes. That's all good and true. But I've heard few military scholars note that the whole David-versus-Goliath confrontation was also one of the first recorded instances of some serious trash-talking as well.

The Bible tells us that Goliath saw the boy coming down the hill and he immediately laid into him, telling him that he planned to kill him and give his flesh "to the birds in the air and the beasts of the field."

David, bless him, did not back down. He gave it back to the giant like a kid from the 'hood, saying that while Goliath might have had a sword, a spear, and a javelin, he had "the name of the Lord Almighty" on his side. Fired up, the shepherd-turned-warrior then really let the giant have it: "This day the LORD will hand you over to me, and I'll strike you down and cut off your head. Today I will give the carcasses of the Philistine army to the birds of the air and the beasts of the earth, and the whole world will know that there is a God in Israel" (I Samuel 17:46).

David then demonstrated what can happen once a Christian soldier is convinced that God has his back. He ran at Goliath and as he went, he took one of the round stones from his bag, put it in his sling, and fired it at the giant. That single stone struck Goliath in one of the few places not protected by his bronze armor—the forehead—and the big guy went down! David then made good on his promise, using Goliath's own sword to finish him off. When the Philistine army saw their champion was dead, they fled with the soldiers from Israel and Judah in pursuit.

It's interesting that some modern-day scientists have speculated as to how David's single stone managed to bring down the mighty Goliath. It's been suggested that the size of Goliath and his family members was caused by acromegaly, a pituitary disorder in which too much human growth hormone is secreted. One of the common side effects of this is soft bone tissue, which might explain why Goliath wore so much armor as well as why a single stone to the forehead might have brought him down. But even if that diagnosis is true, it does not take God out of the equation. For surely God brought the shepherd boy to that battleground and put the stone in his sling for a divine purpose.

Young David was ready, willing, and able to step up when all the other soldiers in the Israeli force were not, because he truly believed that God had his back! The soldiers surely thought of themselves as men of faith, but the only one there who truly had faith was David. The Lord God Almighty brought this boy to the battleground as an example of the purest form of Christian faith. Through the story of David and Goliath and the psalms of David, that lesson has been handed down for thousands of years. Reflect again on his words in Psalm 27: "The LORD is the stronghold of my life—of whom shall I be afraid?"

David lived his faith through a personal relationship with God Jehovah. And he did it as if his life depended upon it! We build our relationships with God by having a regular prayer life and talking with God every day. We build that personal relationship through prayer. And we build trust in him because we have seen him be faithful in other situations. He expresses it again in Proverbs 18:10, saying that the name of the Lord is "a strong tower; the righteous run to it and are safe." David's battle with Goliath is thought to have occurred around 990 BC, nearly a thousand years before Jesus walked on earth. So the boy who would become king of Israel put his life on the line purely on faith alone. You and I have never seen Jesus in the flesh either, but here we are in the twenty-first century, living our lives with the same faith in the Son of God, Jesus Christ. Trusting in his goodness and love, and knowing that it will see us through our challenges.

Get that image of the "strong tower" in your mind. Our Christian faith is a strong tower that we live within. Our belief in Jesus Christ as our savior is our salvation. We have faith. We have conviction. We fear not because even though we cannot see God, we walk by faith, not by sight! And in some cases, we even leap out of airplanes and survive because of the grace of God!

༈

Know that the LORD is God. It is he who made us, and we are his; we are his people, the sheep of his pasture. Enter his gates with thanksgiving and his courts with praise; give thanks to him and praise his name. For the LORD is good and his love endures forever; his faithfulness continues through all generations.

—PSALM 100:3–5

༈

FIVE

Without God's Love, We Have No Love at All!

GOSPEL OF LOVE:

God is the source of all love

"For God so loved the world that he gave his one
and only Son, that whoever believes in him shall not
perish but have eternal life."

—JOHN 3:16

I was still using my real name, Walter Shaw, on the air in 1969,
but just before I started work at Top 40 powerhouse KILT in
Houston, the station program director Bill Young suggested
that I come up with something else. They already had a deejay
whose on-air name was Rick Shaw. (Hold the Asian mode of
transportation jokes, please.)

"Who do you want to be?" Young asked.

What a question! Here was an open invitation to reinvent
myself. The tradition of radio deejays in the rock 'n' roll era
was to cultivate a wild-child image like that of the Moon Dog,
a.k.a. Alan Freed, or Wolfman Jack, whose real name was much

tamer—Bob Smith. The radio waves danced to the rantings of deejay "personalities" with names like Woo-Woo, Poppa Stoppa, Cousin Brucie, Hound Dog, Jocko, Daddy-O, and Martha Jean the Queen.

So if I was going to be part of this colorful carnival, what was I to call myself? I was still a young guy and far from a saint, but I made no pretensions of being part of the drug culture that was so pervasive in the music and broadcast industry at the time. Still, it was also the era of peace and love and the civil rights movement. Since my image was more mellow than most, it made sense when I suggested that I use "love" in my radio name. I liked it also because it wouldn't offend my Christian family members, and he agreed because he was known as a born-again Christian in the industry, where he was well respected because of his no-nonsense lifestyle.

The station created jingles introducing me to listeners as "Walt Love" and that was my on-air name initially. But one night, Steve Lundy, the deejay whose show led into mine, finished his broadcast by playing the Supremes' song "Baby Love." As the last strains of that classic played, he was inspired to introduce me as "Walt 'Baby' Love" and it stuck. The name became a recognized brand in broadcasting, one that advertisers and listeners could easily remember, and I liked the image it gave me. It enabled me to play all sorts of music, including gospel, which is my favorite because it connects me to my Christian roots.

I wish that taking "Love" as part of my on-air name had the effect of automatically making me a more loving and godly person off the air too, but I'm afraid I've had to work at that like everyone else. I have not always succeeded in walking the talk in that regard. But just having "love" in my broadcast name has made me more aware of the importance of it in both my public and private lives. I've been blessed in love, in that I know that my family and my God love me. But my greatest fortune is that I understand that God is the source of all love and his love is the foundation for Christians to build upon.

Cast in Stone

In Matthew 22:37, we're told that Jesus believed the two greatest commandments were, first of all, to love the Lord your God with all your heart and with all your soul and with all your mind; and second, to love your neighbor as yourself. God's commandments are serious business, considering that they are the basis of most of mankind's civil and social law. Yet in the secular world, the term *love* gets thrown around haphazardly, especially by Madison Avenue and the media. Obviously, we need more of God's sincere love and less of the shallow sort found on Valentine's candy and reality television shows. It's safe to say that many people have lost track of what love truly means in a society where more than 50 percent of marriages end in divorce. Many people simply have no foundation for understanding it because they don't know love in its purest form: *God's love.*

No Greater Love

As a Christian, I know that God is love. His word tells me so in I John 4:16. "And so we know and rely on the love God has for us. God is love. Whoever lives in love lives in God, and God in him." The Apostle John had a lot to say about love in his writings and teachings. He was also called "Saint John the Evangelist" and "Saint John the Theologian" and the "preacher of divine love."

As the youngest of the apostles, John, the son of Zebedee, a fisherman from Galilee, and his wife Salome, was like a beloved little brother to Jesus. He is often described as the most inno-cent, loving, and pure of the twelve chosen disciples. His posi-tion as a favorite of Jesus was such that it is believed that Jesus, while dying on the cross, was referring to John when he gave directions for the care of his mother. John 19:26–27 tells us that Jesus looked down and saw his mother "and the disciple whom he loved standing nearby, he said to his mother, 'Dear woman, here is your son,' and to the disciple, 'Here is your mother.' From that time on, this disciple took her into his home."

We're told that after Jesus died, was resurrected, and as-cended into heaven, John went to Rome to preach the gospel and was tortured there before moving to Ephesus, a center for learning located in what is now Turkey. It is also where the Apostle Paul eventually settled. John founded many Christian church communities in the region in the years that followed. Late in his life, this champion of Christian love was captured by the Roman emperor Domitian, a pagan who persecuted Christians. Domitian's soldiers took John to Rome where he was tried for being a Christian and preaching about Jesus. He was then beaten, poisoned, and thrown into a tub of boiling oil. Yet God apparently had more work for John to do on earth, because he survived! Domitian was so stunned that John survived such torment that he was afraid that God might bring down his wrath on him if he killed him, so Domitian exiled him to the Greek island Patmos. A short time later, Domitian was murdered and all of his exiles were forgiven by his successor. So John, who lived into his nineties, returned to spend the rest of his long life in Ephesus.

The torture, beatings, and boiling in oil did not weaken John's capacity for love or his belief in its power. We're told that while visiting a Christian church near the town of Smyrna, John was so impressed with an intelligent young boy that he asked the church's bishop to look after his religious education and welfare personally. But the bishop eventually lost track of the boy, who fell in with a bad crowd. Because of his intelligence, he became the leader of a notorious gang of thieves. When the apostle returned to Smyrna, he asked the bishop about the boy he'd left in his charge. The bishop had to confess that he'd lost track of the boy and he'd become a notorious thief who hid out in the surrounding mountains. You have to like Saint John and the almighty power of his love for his fellow man. He was no longer a young guy. He'd been reviled, exiled, and tortured. Yet we're told that his first words to the bishop were: "Give me a horse and a guide."

John rode off in search of a lost soul, armed only with the love that his Christian beliefs and the Son of God had willed to him. He'd only ridden a short way into the foothills when the thief's gang jumped him and took him captive. John demanded to be taken to their leader. They obeyed the old man, who seemed powerful despite his years. Their leader recognized him and his power too. As soon as he saw John, the apostle who had lovingly tried to cultivate his gifts for good purposes, the thief turned to run from him. John followed him, telling him that he could still find "hope in salvation."

The thief continued to flee until Saint John unleashed his most powerful weapon, his unconditional love: "I would willingly die for you, just as Christ died for us. I would give my soul for you."

That did it. The thief turned back to John and embraced him, asking for his forgiveness. John then dropped to his knees and prayed for God's forgiveness for the boy-turned-thief. The power of his Christian love became legendary and even into his advanced old age, John continued his missionary work to gatherings of the faithful.

One of John's final teachings was simply: "Children, love one another!" We're told John said this over and over and then added, "This is the command of the Lord, and if you fulfill it, it is sufficient."

Scripture offers many verses from John that provide perspective on God's love. The three verses leading up to verse 16 (1 John 4:13–15) are particularly inspiring:

> We know that we live in him and he in us, because he has given us of his Spirit. And we have seen and testify that the Father has sent his Son to be the Savior of the world. If anyone acknowledges that Jesus is the Son of God, God lives in him and he in God.

Tough Love

Hold on to those thoughts from the Apostle John and I guarantee your life will get better. Your personal relationship with Jesus is the key to your salvation, and how you apply his love and your Christian beliefs in your own relationships is the key to your happiness on this earth. I've seen it put to the test in the real world. Before my mother passed and went to the Lord, I made a trip home to see her in western Pennsylvania over a long weekend. She was suffering from lupus and I knew the effects of lupus were wearing her down.

While I was visiting my ailing mother I received a long-distance telephone call from my girlfriend—this was many years before I got married. I really cared deeply for this woman, but at that point I was upset with her. She had backed out of coming with me because some childhood friends from her native Trinidad had decided to come visit her. When she called, I didn't curse at her or shout at her, but I was very short with her and dismissive of her efforts to make amends. My mother was listening. She had met this girlfriend once and was fond of her. So when I got off the telephone, I got some late-stage parental guidance. (You know how mothers are.) She gave me a shot of humility, or, as the old folks might say, she put me in my place. And my mother didn't believe in gentle persuasion.

She reached up, grabbed my shirt, and twisted it in her motherly little hand. "Listen to me, Walter," she said. "You know better than to conduct yourself like that! Don't you ever let me hear you talk to anyone like that ever again. You should also understand that I have to love you because God gave you to me. But I don't have to like you!"

Boy, was she angry with me. With that she gave me a forceful shove in the chest and strolled back into her living room like I wasn't even there. My mother didn't play around. Mothers know which buttons to push on their children because they installed them. And she was pushing mine, for sure. She'd not had an easy life, but as she grew older and mellowed, she was a compassionate, loving, and kind woman. And if she saw that you were in need of some tough love, look out! As sick as she was, she could still dish it out in no uncertain terms. She offered me a lesson in unconditional love that I never forgot. She awoke the Holy Spirit in me, which is the voice of our conscience, and she reminded me that I was not conducting myself as the Christian I was raised to be. She reminded me that Christians are kind and loving and forgiving and more thoughtful of their friends than I was being. Thank you, Jesus, for my mother's tough love, because I know it was the product of her unconditional love—God's love. And if we didn't have God's love, sometimes we would have no other love at all!

The manner in which I spoke to my girlfriend was unworthy of a Christian. I was out of line, off base, and too full of myself. Some of y'all know what I'm talking about if you're willing to tell the truth. It's difficult to look in the mirror and admit to yourself what a jerk you are sometimes. God's spirit used my mother at a critical point in my life. My ego runneth over at that point. It happens. I was in my late twenties and I'd made it through some very rough and tough challenges in the military. I'd started my radio career near the very bottom and, at that point, my hard work had begun to produce some results. I wasn't aware of it, but I'd crossed the fine line from confidence to arrogance. Without realizing it, I'd fallen into the ego trap, thinking I was all that and then some.

Living Love

Executive recruiters say that one of the most valued assets that top managers look for in choosing their future leaders is "the ability to self-correct." That sounds so basic, doesn't it? Yet how many of us have that ability to realize—without being hit up-side the head—that we're barreling down the wrong path, that we've made some bad decisions, that our attitudes need adjust-ment, or our approaches are out of step or ineffective? I think that rare ability to self-correct is also known by another term: wisdom.

I certainly knew better than to treat another person the way I had treated my girlfriend on the telephone. I wasn't wise enough to see it until my mother put it in my face. I was dou-bly embarrassed because as a Christian believer, I have no ex-cuse for losing my humility and for lacking grace. I know that I have God's unconditional love, which is the source of all love and wisdom too.

One of the most interesting of Jesus' disciples, the Apostle Paul, who had been a persecutor of Christians before his legendary conversion, offers great wisdom on love in his writings and speeches as recorded in the Bible. In I Corinthians 13:4–8, he says:

> *Love is patient, love is kind. It does not envy, it does not boast, it is not proud. It is not rude, it is not self-seeking, it is not easily angered, it keeps no record of wrongs. Love does not delight in evil but rejoices with the truth. It always protects, always trusts, always hopes, always perseveres. Love never fails.*

That's beautiful and inspiring, isn't it? But Paul could crack the whip too. He was a man of conviction who believed in walking the talk in whatever he believed. Even before he be-came a Christian through God's own intervention, Paul lived his beliefs. He was born around the year 10 B.C., in what is now the southern coastal area of Turkey, in the city of Tarsus. His

parents were Roman citizens and Jews, which was a little unusual as non-Italians were granted the honor of citizenship in
the empire only if they had great influence and wealth. Paul
was sent to Jerusalem at the age of fourteen to be trained as a
rabbi and, since these were pragmatic people, also as a tent
maker so he could pay the bills. As a young man of deep con-
victions who believed in living them, Paul had no tolerance for
what he regarded as heresy against his Jewish beliefs, so when
he thought others—the Christian followers of Jesus Christ—
were practicing it, he became their worst nightmare. He was
known for going door to door to drag Christians out of their
homes and to jail. He was headed for Damascus, on a mission
to attack Christians, when God intervened and converted him.

Paul had strong feelings about loving Jesus and also about
how Christians must live their faith. He tells us in Romans
12:2–3 how we ought to behave as Christians. So there are no
excuses. Paul tells us:

> Do not conform any longer to the pattern of this world, but be trans-
> formed by the renewing of your mind. Then you will be able to test and
> approve what God's will is—his good, pleasing and perfect will. For by
> the grace given me I say to every one of you: Do not think of yourself
> more highly than you ought, but rather think of yourself with sober
> judgment, in accordance with the measure of faith God has given you.

Lessons in Love

Sometimes it is downright scary how the words of the Bible seem to be directed at you and your situation, isn't it? The words come flying off those pages like spears aimed at your heart. *Do not think of yourself more highly than you ought.* It's humbling to think that my bigheaded pigheadedness was being addressed thousands of years ago by one of Jesus' chosen disciples.

Of course, it would be egocentric to think that Saint Paul sat down at his writing desk with the thought, *Walter Shaw is going to need a lesson in faith and humility one of these days, so I'd better come up with something catchy.* No, the humbling part of finding such an on-point lesson in the Bible is that my failings are nothing special. They are common for humans. That is why God sent his Son to us, to atone for the common sins of common men and women. And that is why the words of the Bible were written, to make sure the lessons he taught were not forgotten. The Bible is God's self-help book. It tells us how to live our lives better and how to be more productive in this world while always acknowledging God's love for us.

After apologizing to my mother, I crawled back to the kitchen with my tail between my legs, and made my "please forgive me" long-distance telephone call to my girlfriend back in Yonkers. In reflection, I can see that because I'd fulfilled manly duties in the military and in the work world, I thought I *was* a man. In truth, I was only playing at being a man. I hadn't earned the title yet. I certainly wasn't conducting myself or living my life as a godly man. I needed a lot of godly work. It is a life's work. No Christian can afford to rest on his or her laurels. We don't become believers and then coast to our divine rewards. It's one long, hard but glorious trek, and it is fueled by

God's love for his flawed, often foolish, and sometimes full-of-themselves creations.

Ultimate Love

The ultimate story of unconditional love and forgiveness, of course, is that of Jesus Christ and his willingness to die on the cross for our sins and thereby give us eternal life. John 3:16 shows God's ultimate love for us as his creations gone bad. Scripture says, "For God so loved the world that he gave his one and only Son, that whoever believes in him shall not perish but have eternal life." I'm always touched by stories of God's unconditional love, perhaps because I received so much of it from my great-grandparents and other members of my extended family as a child. It didn't seem unusual at the time, but when I reflect on my boyhood, my circumstances were unusual, and I think they left me with a real appreciation for unconditional love. The absence of my natural mother and father might have left me feeling unloved, except for all the affection I received from the family members who stepped up and gave me a home in their hearts.

Unconditional love from family members is not something that should be taken for granted. My childhood could have been miserable given the fact that I did not live with my mother and father, but as it worked out, I benefited from the unconditional love of an entire extended family. Yet I also received a far more unusual form of unconditional love in the military, of all places. It came from an unlikely source, Master Sergeant Russell T. Barnes. Sergeant Barnes already had nearly thirty years of military service by the time I showed up in his outfit. He was probably nearly sixty years old, but he had forearms like Popeye and could knock out push-ups for hours at a time. He was a fantastic soldier who'd been a member of the first black paratrooper unit, the 555th Parachute Infantry Battalion, also known as the "Triple Nickel."

Master Sergeant Barnes was a proud soldier and a solid Christian who demanded excellence from his men, especially the young black men who came under his supervision. He pulled me aside early in my training, as he did many other black guys, and let me know what was coming: "I am going to be tougher on you than anyone else because I demand excellence from you." It was his form of tough love, but it was truly unconditional love. He wanted us to succeed and he challenged us while also giving us the tools to meet the challenges he laid down. Master Sergeant Barnes had lived with racism in the military, which was pervasive, and he was determined that it would be overcome by sheer excellence.

"There are still some white guys in the army who think you will be slow, lazy, and shiftless, but that's not going to happen on my watch," he told me.

There were some black guys who didn't respond to his tough love. I was a country guy who was used to camping and hunting and long treks. But a lot of the city guys who acted tough weren't up for the strenuous standards and principles established by Master Sergeant Barnes. But I loved that sort of challenge, and I came to love him because he made me a better soldier and a better man.

There are many examples of Christian soldiers and unconditional love in the Bible. One of the most compelling involves David, the future King of Israel. This story comes after his slaying of Goliath but before David became a great leader. We're told that King Saul wanted David killed because his fame as a warrior began to overshadow Saul's own stature. Saul's efforts to kill David were thwarted by his own son Jonathan, who was a close friend of David. In I Samuel 19:1–4, Jonathan tells David to be on his guard and to go into hiding so that he can intercede by talking to his father.

The Bible teaches that Jonathan was very loyal to his father and also to David. But his first loyalty was to God. We must first be loyal to God, and his love in us will then help us to earn the loyalty of others. "We love because he first loved us," according to I John 4:19.

Today as the father of two sons, I'm both the recipient and the giver of unconditional love. And as a minister and recipient of a master of arts degree in theology, I'm a student of its presence throughout the Bible. Here's a blessing from the Bible about love. It's found in Romans 12:9–10: "Love must be sincere. Hate what is evil; cling to what is good. Be devoted to one another in brotherly love. Honor one another above yourselves."

That inspiring passage in Romans also encourages us to zealously serve the Lord, to be "joyful in hope, patient in affliction, and faithful in prayer." It is really a guide to living like a Christian, advising believers to share with those in need, to be hospitable, to bless and not curse those who persecute us, and to practice empathy with others whether they are rejoicing or mourning.

Love the Needy

Whenever I read this part of Romans, I feel refreshed by its messages to live in harmony with others, free of pride and willing to reach out to those in the lowest realms—especially since I grew up in those "lowest realms." Christians need to remember that Jesus sought out the poorest and neediest sinners as the most important members of his flock. In these days of mega-churches and ministries with their own fleets of private jets, it is important to share the wealth of God's blessings and to continue the work of Jesus Christ on earth.

The fifty-square-block Skid Row neighborhood in downtown Los Angeles is one of those places where Christian charity that expresses God's unconditional love is most needed. It is said to be the largest service-dependent ghetto in the nation, one in which 11,000 residents—85 percent of them black and 80 percent male—live often desperate existences. Even amid an array of missions, shelters, drop-ins, and single-room-occupancy hotels, an estimated 4,000 live on streets and sidewalks that have thirty times the bacterial contamination of raw sewage, according to one city report.

At least 70 percent of L.A.'s Skid Row residents have histories of drug or alcohol abuse and one-third are mentally ill, according to social service agencies. Crime, disease, drugs, vice, and violence are part of day-to-day life there. It is not by chance that so many of the poor and needy end up here. For thirty-five years, the City of Los Angeles has had a policy of "containment" to provide services for the underclass in one area of shelters, missions, transient hotels, and social services.

Every time I go to Skid Row to take part in some sort of Christian charity, I realize how blessed I am and how we as a society need to do more for those who have fallen on hard times. The fact is, there is a much finer line these days between those who are contributing to society and those who are dependent upon it. High rates of debt and the volatile employment market can swiftly make dependents of almost anyone. Nothing could be more humbling, or frightening.

In late 2005, I spoke at a ceremony in memory of those homeless and low-income residents who had passed away on Skid Row that year. It was held in San Julian Park on a cool but sunny Southern California day. I'd been to this park on several occasions to participate in outreach efforts to the homeless on behalf of my church, the First A.M.E. Church, Los Angeles, which has eighteen thousand members and the ability to do a lot of good work for those in need. On previous occasions, our outreach was very basic. We distributed items such as clothes, new shoes, and essentials like toothpaste, lotions, and shampoo. We've also distributed many Bibles there over the years. The event to remember those who passed in 2005 was a different sort of outreach. It offered an intimate look into the lives of the area's residents. They came to remember the friends they'd lost in lives marked by losses and suffering of the deepest kind. These people dwell at the bottom of America's socioeconomic structure and it was heartbreaking to see them grieving yet another blow. It's become a media cliché to refer to them as the faceless and forgotten, or the people who've "fallen through the cracks." It is our Christian duty to look into those faces and to address their suffering so they are not forgotten. Proverbs 31:9 says: "Speak up and judge fairly; defend the rights of the poor and needy." God expects Christians to reach out and help these people return to productive lives. They too are God's children.

Over the years, I've met many who run and work for organizations that provide services to the residents of Skid Row. Theirs is difficult, sometimes thankless work, yet they exhibit a grace that comes only from serving God by serving his people. Some of those who now help the needy were once on the other side of the serving line. They understand, as all of us should, that yet by the grace of God, we could be the ones living in this hell on earth. Every time I go into Skid Row, I am humbled by the efforts of those who spend their days and nights serving the needy there.

During the memorial ceremony, I met two Los Angeles police officers, Patrol Division Captain Jodi Wakefield and Senior Lead Officer Kathy McAnany. Their compassion for the residents of Skid Row also reminded me that stereotypes about police officers also can be way off base. Before the event's program began, Officer McAnany and several others involved in the neighborhood were talking about residents they knew who had passed away that year. Officer McAnany recognized that one woman's "street name" was listed on the program, and she noted that her real name was Debra. The policewoman expressed sorrow for this woman's death, noting that she had befriended her and always checked on her to make sure she was okay. Her compassion touched me. Officer McAnany is a supervisor responsible for the safety of other men and women in her division, yet she had made the effort to know the homeless and needy under their care too. It also impressed me that she knew the homeless woman's real name and history, and she wanted to make sure that everyone in charge knew that her real name was Debra. It was a small gesture, but it revealed this police officer's concern for others. I kept my program from that event as inspiration to remember both the people in need and those who serve them. I was blessed that day because God wanted me to see those Christian beliefs in action. To God be the glory!

When I left Skid Row that afternoon, as always, I was counting my many blessings and thanking God from the bottom of my heart. When you see, feel, hear, and interact with such misery, pain, sorrow, and despair, it impacts you. I am always struck by the fact that there is such a fine line between "making it" as a productive member of this society and not making it as someone living on the street, or in a jail cell. That reality gets in your face when you get to know the residents of Skid Row.

As I drove home on that particular day, God's Spirit joined me in the car and inspired me to start humming the gospel tune, "He Laid His Hands on Me." It is one of those pieces from way back, a spiritual dating to the time of slavery and probably well before. It is one of those heart-gripping hymns that speaks to your soul. It always makes me reflect on how lucky I am to experience God's love and blessings. I'll be truthful. It always makes me teary-eyed with joy and gratitude. I visualized myself singing in the congregation at First A.M.E. Church in Los Angeles with Pastor John. Before I knew it, I was singing out loud in my car with tears streaming down my cheeks and dripping onto my blue dress shirt. The Lord laid his hands on me in that moment. That is the power of God's love as expressed in his music!

Power of Love

God the Father's messages flow from the Bible with advice to remain humble, avoid evil ways, do what is right, and live in peace with your neighbors. Some of it is easier to read and appreciate than to put into action in everyday life. "Do not take revenge, my friends, but leave room for God's wrath," is one bit of Romans that we struggle with. But you have to admire the attitude that comes with the encouragement to feed and give drink to your enemies: "In doing this, you will heap burning coals on his head."

Overcoming evil through unconventional love and goodness may sound Pollyanna-ish in a cynical and often cruel world, but then consider that some of modern-day man's greatest accomplishments came through application of that very principle based on God's unconditional love for mankind. We all have to learn to become more Christlike in the way we conduct our lives. Quite frankly, we have to learn to deny ourselves our wishes, our wants, and our desires in life. We've got to strive for God's will in our lives instead of the creature comforts we seek. God would have us do the right thing at all times. Obviously, we can't do it all by ourselves. But, glory hallelujah! With God's Holy Spirit we can do much better because we can be transformed by the renewing of our minds.

Love One Another

The key to living in Christ is to look for God's presence in each other and to love all of God's people accordingly. It takes a true loving, Christian heart to throw aside stereotypes and personal biases and racial and class distinctions to see God in all people. Regardless of where we stand on the socioeconomic ladder, we are all servants and disciples of God. And we must do as Jesus said, we must love one another.

"A new command I give you: Love one another. As I have loved you, so you must love one another. By this all men will know that you are my disciples, if you love one another" (John 13:34–35).

Jesus makes this statement after he has washed the feet of the apostles and just as he is telling them, mysteriously, that one of them will betray him soon and that he is about to go to a place where they cannot follow now but they will follow later—to his death on the cross and his resurrection into heaven. The apostles are feeling a little dazed and confused at all this. First, there is the whole strange scene of Jesus, their leader, wanting to wash their feet. Some of them are embarrassed by this act. It is the act of a servant, and that was Jesus' purpose. He wanted to leave them with a true model of love as expressed by humility and service to others. And he wanted them to love one another just as he had loved them. He is about to give up his life in service to his Father and to them and all mankind.

Jesus shared his divine love with his apostles. As he prepared his disciples for his final days, he was directing them to go out and share it with all God's people on earth. Let's look again at the quote from John 3:16 at the beginning of this chapter: "For God so loved the world that he gave his one and only Son, that whoever believes in him shall not perish but have eternal life."

Jesus was calling for his disciples to form a united front

with each other, with him and with God the Father. He was preparing for his final mission on earth, and he was preparing them to continue with their work as missionaries to spread the word of his death and resurrection. The apostles were about to face some serious tests of their own faith. They would question themselves individually. They would be challenged by others. By calling for them to love each other and all of mankind, Jesus was giving them a source of strength to meet the challenges ahead. God's love is essential. Without it, we are empty vessels. I encourage you to never take it for granted and to pray in gratitude for more of it at every opportunity. Love and faith cannot exist without each other, and we cannot live as Christians without them both.

꒐

The Son is the radiance of God's glory and the exact representation of his being, sustaining all things by his powerful word.
—HEBREWS 1:3

꒐

SIX

Living in His Light

GOSPEL OF LOVE:
Hold On to Hope

Always be prepared to give an answer to everyone
who asks you to give the reason for the hope that
you have.

—1 PETER 3:15

I was diagnosed with kidney cancer in late October of 1996.
My doctors said I had a 70 percent chance of dying, but if I
underwent surgery to remove the "bad" kidney, it improved to
a 50/50 chance of living depending on whether the cancer had
spread. My great-grandfather died of kidney cancer and my father had kidney cancer, so it didn't take a lot of convincing for
me to do whatever I could to improve my chances. I told the
doctors that over the years I've grown very accustomed to living
so I'd like to keep at it for a while longer.

I was fifty-four at the time of the diagnosis. Like everyone,
I know I will die someday. And like everyone, too, I want to
put off the inevitable as long as I can. The Bible offers many

accounts of people who are said to be more than one hundred years old. But even good Christians have no right to longevity. So when the word *cancer* came up, I felt extremely vulnerable particularly because of my family history. To calm my nerves, I recalled my great-grandmother's example. She believed that there is great healing power in prayer. She taught me how to pray as a boy and I've been praying ever since. I was four or five years old and I remember my great-grandmother Susie would kneel down next to me beside the bed and tell me to put my hands together to pray. And we would pray: "Now I lay me down to sleep. I pray the Lord my soul to keep. If I should die before I wake, I pray the Lord my soul to take." Then in the morning we would pray and thank God for getting us through the night. And we would pray at breakfast to thank God for giving us food to eat. And my great-grandparents would pray before my great-grandfather walked out the door. My great-grandmother would pray for God to keep him safe. I saw that all my life, so prayer was part of my life and I prayed before, during, and after football games, basketball games, tests, and every other important event in my day.

In the four gospels of the Bible, the disciples ask Jesus to teach them to pray and he said: "Our Father who art in heaven." And that is how Jesus taught his disciples to pray. You pray by communicating with God.

Along with her unconditional love and the example of her faith in God, my great-grandmother's gift of prayer was one of the most blessed things she did for me. My mother chipped in by advising me to "be specific" when I pray. "Ask God for what you want," she'd say. The Bible tells us that God already knows what we need. But as one of the gospel songs says, it is important to go before the Lord, humble ourselves on our knees, and tell him of our troubles and our wants.

Focus on Good

My mother also told me to focus on the good in every situation rather than the bad. Her rationale was that God's view of things is much different from our human perspective. I've come to appreciate her wisdom on that point more and more as I've studied the Bible more intensely for seminary school and as an ordained minister and elder. What we see as bad from our limited view may actually be a very positive thing from the Creator's greater vantage point. After all, we have a very narrow perspective, while God holds the whole world in his hands.

I've come to see that this truth applied even to my frightening bout with kidney cancer. Jesus wisely warned us that we would face challenges in our earthly lives. Our Lord and Savior made that statement on his way to Jerusalem to be crucified. He was teaching his disciples how to pray in his name as if in a conversation with him. We all feel abandoned at times in our lives. Right or wrong, we feel that those we love and trust are blind to our predicaments and our fears. I've been through it, and I'm sure you have too. Such trials are part of our passage on earth. Whether you've lost someone you love or simply lost your way, the solution is the same. Look to our Savior Jesus Christ for guidance.

There are many blessings to be found in the Bible and many wise and inspiring words. Yet I'm particularly thankful every time I come upon the common word *but* in my Bible readings. Why? Because often when God says "but," it leads to an uplifting message of hope and encouragement. That simple word serves as a portal for hopefulness even in troubling times. Scripture says in John 16:33: "I have told you these things, so that in me you may have peace. In this world you will have trouble. *But* take heart! I have overcome the world."

Christians must grow in Christ so we understand that our peace is found through him and his love. These gifts will help see us through all the difficult times. Jesus fought the ultimate battle and won. Our trials and tribulations may seem overwhelming, *but* scripture tells us that our peace is found in him. No matter how bad things may look, child of God, you've got to learn to trust the Lord. Even Jesus in his human form had to learn to trust Father God to raise him from the dead on the third day. Our Lord and Savior conquered death when he was willing to die on the cross for our sins. Always, our faith and our hope are in Jesus.

Cancer Countdown

Still, life can sneak up on us and slap us silly. In those situations, we sometimes fail to recall the power of our faith and hope in the Lord God. It certainly happened to me when cancer came calling. It was a Tuesday night and I was with the production staff for one of my syndicated shows, *The Countdown with Walt "Baby" Love.* Each Tuesday night we would record that show and interview our live guests for that week's program. On this occasion, everything was going well. I was in a great mood, the staff was in fine form, and the show was clicking along like clockwork.

It's just eerie how something as mundane as a bathroom

break can bring high drama into your life. That's what happened in this case. I will spare you the graphic details, but it was not a routine trip to the men's room. Something was obviously wrong. I did not ignore the signs and, please, don't let anyone you love ignore theirs. The devil wants us to be blind to God's warning signs, but as Christians we defy the devil and act when our Lord Jesus Christ sends a call to action.

Initially, I froze with fear when I saw blood where blood should not be. I was well aware of the history of kidney cancer in my family and though I'd felt no pain, I immediately suspected the worst. *Oh, my God! I've got cancer.* I couldn't move. My mind was racing with thoughts of what I needed to do, who I needed to see, the plans and dreams that I'd yet to carry out. I panicked. Then I panicked some more. It was 10:00 P.M., so I fought back the urge to call my physician and demand an immediate appointment. I did ask God what he was doing to me. But in my shock and fear, I did not pray as much as I should have. My faith was overrun by my panic.

Finally, I pulled myself together and went back into the studio. Members of my staff teased me for the long bathroom break: "Man, we thought you fell in. We were going to send a search party."

Only Diana, my writer and producer, noticed that my mood was somber.

"Are you all right? You don't look good. Did something happen? You look pale to me," she said.

Her woman's intuition had kicked in. Even when I tried to hide my concerns and carry on with the show, she saw through the act. I could not get revved up with the necessary energy and enthusiasm. It had also dawned on me that the next day I was scheduled to take a 6:00 A.M. flight from Los Angeles to Chicago. I had to be there for an extremely important meeting with one of the largest advertising agencies in the country. Their buyers wanted to meet me face-to-face before sealing a very lucrative deal with me. They'd planned a party for me. We were counting on this sale to go through, so I had to be there, and I had to be enthusiastic, energized, charming, focused, and mentally sharp. I could not be panicked, distracted, or sickly.

Still, I did not pray as I should have. All of my Christian training and encouragement failed to kick in because I was so focused on despair and grief and the worst possible scenarios. At that point, I had no hope, only fear. My mind was racing with fearful thoughts: *What am I going to do? What about my family? My children? My business?*

I went on autopilot so we could finish recording the show and then I got out of there. At that point, everyone knew something was wrong so they did what they could to get me on my way. My drive home to the 'burbs was even longer than usual. I talked to myself and I talked to God. *Yet still I did not pray as I should have!*

Heavenly Alert

Fear and panic had given way to Baby Love befuddlement. My mind was on overload. So many thoughts were flying around in there it must have looked like a ticker-tape parade on Wall Street. Or *Walt* Street! I was dazed and confused. Beat up and knocked out. Lost and still losing it!

But did I pray? No, I did not.

As a broadcasting veteran it should have hit me sooner that this was the heavenly version of the Emergency Broadcast System. How many times had I heard *that?*

"*This is a test. For the next sixty seconds, this station will conduct a test of the Emergency Broadcast System. This is only a test.*"

Yes, the Lord Jesus Christ was testing me and my faith in the power of his love—the Christian Emergency God-cast System, if you will. So it was only a test, and I was flunking big time. God had sent me through the hot flames of fear so he could alter and change my Christian chemistry while refining me, and I would really know that he was God—and God all by himself! It was going to be the way God wanted it to be. Not how I wanted it to be, or how I thought it should be.

It was midnight when I got home. My family was sleeping. My suitcases were waiting, packed for the business trip to Chicago. I was supposed to leave for the airport in four hours. But I couldn't sleep. I had an inner debate about calling my doctor. I made feeble attempts to calm myself between moments of sheer panic and despair. I tried to tell myself I was overreacting. Blood in the urine can be a sign of all sorts of minor illnesses or problems, right? Maybe it was just an infection or a kidney stone. I'd been a football player and a paratrooper; maybe it was just an old injury flaring.

King of Denial

The devil will mess up your mind if you let him. He'll cast you into darkness and blind you to all hope unless you seek God's light. I was stumbling, bumping into walls, and fumbling in the black shadows of depression. I was a good example of a bad example. I turned inward in my despair instead of looking upward with hope.

Don't shut down! Open up! Look for God's love and listen for the voice of the Holy Spirit. I had tuned out any voice but the guttural urgings of the dark angel. But finally, the Holy Spirit who guards and guides us broke through my mental fog, telling me: *"Wake up your wife. Tell her what has happened. Call your doctor. Forget the flight to Chicago. It can wait! This can't!"*

But did I listen? Did I heed the heavenly voice? Did I tap into my Christian training and get down on my knees for a conversation with the Lord God Our Father and ask for his guidance and mercy?

Of course not. The fog only thickened. I'd been nervously drinking water, which had the natural effect, and this time there were no ominous signs. I took that as an indication that everything must be A-OK and that what had happened before was just an anomaly. (You can call me the King of Denial, it's okay.)

I left my house without waking anyone. My panic subsided. I was relieved. I felt as though I'd dodged a bullet. Did I check in with the man upstairs? No, I was too busy taking care of my earthly business to do that. At 3:00 A.M., I drove to the Los Angeles airport, and the only thing on my mind was concern that some overzealous lawman would see my face behind the wheel of my Jaguar and pull me over for DWB (driving while black), which is not at all unusual in Southern California. But it didn't happen. Another bullet dodged.

My flight was on time. I settled back and tried to relax after drinking some orange juice. Midway through, I went to the restroom and, at 40,000 feet, my panic returned. This time, I called for help. I used the on-board telephone and contacted my doctor's office. I told the receptionist it was an emergency so she put me through to Dr. May. He was calm and reassuring.

"Don't panic. From what you described, it could be a kidney stone," he said.

Dr. May promised to get me in to see a top urologist as soon as I returned the next day. I tried to calm myself and to focus on business for the rest of the flight. Prayer was not part of the program. Instead, I went on autopilot upon landing at O'Hare International Airport. I went to my downtown hotel, met with our salespeople, and headed for the meeting with the advertising representatives. The carefully planned discussions went smoothly. I managed not to scare off the advertisers by screaming out my worst fears about my medical condition. I kept my emotions completely under control. I was Mr. Cool, Mr. Calm, and Mr. Collected.

But once we hit the celebration after the successful meeting, my body did its own thing. An intense fever had me sweating through my suit jacket. Sharp pains jabbed in my right lower back as if someone were punching my kidney and trying to take me out. I'd been in some serious brawls as a teen and in the military, but I'd never felt pain like this. The pain brought me to my knees when my faith had not; in front of my staff and my new business associates at this very prestigious party, I went down in agony.

Medical Maze

Even in my pain, I was panicked that people would think I was drunk or doing drugs. As they escorted me to Northwestern

Memorial Hospital in downtown Chicago, my staff assured me that they'd let everyone know I was dealing with a medical problem. The emergency room nurse tried to put me at ease as she assessed my condition:

"You're a big, strong, good-looking guy. What's wrong with you?"

I had to laugh at her bedside manner and then I filled her in. She thought it sounded like a kidney stone, so she ordered up X-rays of my kidneys. I was hoping for a painkiller. Instead, she administered some more tough love: "All you guys are real babies. That's why women have the kids—because they can take pain. This is the closest you'll get to feeling the pain women have to endure when they go into labor. Now, I want you to quit whining!"

Ah, women! They never miss an opportunity to set men straight. I laughed through the pain and tried not to whine until she was out of earshot. Next came a flurry of nurses and doctors and needles and tubes and X-rays. If you've been through any sort of medical problem, you know the drill. And you know the sense of helplessness you feel wearing that open-backed hospital gown as they shuttle you around, prick, poke, and prod you all night long.

What are good Christians supposed to do when we feel helpless and fearful? I go to the Word of God—the Bible. And then I look for scriptures that have helped me in the past when I've gone through some trial or tribulation in my life. I try and reach back and grab something that I know will help me. If I can't think of anything at the moment, I pray and ask God to have the Holy Spirit illuminate something in his Word for me. At this point I knew enough to dig out three verses of Psalm

121 that had started to become part of my "full armor" of God. The Bible does tell us to put on the "full armor" of God to protect ourselves against the "fiery darts" of the devil when we're under attack from him. Psalm 121:1–2, 7–8 says:

"I lift up my eyes to the hills—where does my help come from? My help comes from the LORD, the Maker of heaven and earth. The LORD will keep you from all harm—he will watch over your life; the LORD will watch over your coming and going both now and forevermore."

We are supposed to look to the Almighty God Our Father in heaven and pray for his grace and blessings! But I was so caught up in all of the medical mumbo jumbo and in the massive jumble of my own fears and confusion that I did not pray as much as I should have! Oh, I might have muttered woeful "Help me, Jesus!" once or twice, but never did I drop down on my knees and put my heart and soul into prayer. In fact, at that point, I'm humbled to say, I was looking as much to the nurses, doctors, and urologists than to heaven for my hope.

Finally, they concluded that there was no more blood in my kidneys. So the next morning the attending physician and I agreed that the best thing to do, since my condition had stabilized, was for me to head back to Los Angeles where my own doctors could investigate further.

Believe me, by this point, Walt Baby Love was holding on to hope in a big way! I was hoping that this would all come down to a little kidney stone that would make its merry way on out of my life and leave me alone. And at first that's what my urologist in Los Angeles seemed to think might happen, too. After doing his own analysis, he determined that we should wait several days and see if I passed a kidney stone. If it didn't come out on its own, he planned to fire up his own Jedi light saber and go in after it. To my relief, all the medical experts seemed to agree that I was not facing a life-threatening situation.

Did I pray then? Did I thank Jesus for delivering me from the specter of the kidney cancer that had taken other members of my family? Yes, I did!

Jaws of Distress

I returned to work and did my best to keep my mind occupied while waiting to see if the kidney stone moved on. It was a strange situation, trying to go on with my normal life while hoping for a sign—even another twinge of pain or the sight of more blood—to let me know that it was only a kidney stone passing through. What's the saying? No pain, no gain? The Bible has that covered, too, of course, in Job 36:15–16:

> But those who suffer he delivers in their suffering; he speaks to them in their affliction. "He is wooing you from the jaws of distress to a spacious place free from restriction, to the comfort of your table laden with choice food."

I don't know for certain that God had brought this trial to me to get my attention. At first, I was so concerned about my physical health that I did not make that spiritual connection. I was very focused on the fact that other members of my family had died from kidney cancer, so it did not occur to me that this was some sort of test or wake-up call. Looking back, I now feel certain that God was speaking to me in my affliction. But at the time, I simply went back to work. When there came no further pain or blood, I was relieved, in a way. But my doctor was not willing to conclude that the earlier warning signs were false alarms.

"I want to take a look and see what is going on in there," he said.

So I put my faith in him and the Lord, and agreed to go under the laser. When I woke up from the procedure, there was an IV in my arm. That seemed ominous. I'd been planning on going home. After all, this was just a look-see as far as I was concerned. My wife was nowhere to be seen, nor was my doctor. Nobody on the staff would answer my questions. Finally, a nurse informed me that my doctor was in surgery and would not be available for five hours. I couldn't leave until I talked to him, she said.

I was not doing a very good job of holding on to hope. I was doing all I could to maintain my grip on sanity. This situation felt all wrong. Finally, my wife came back and asked if I was ready to go. I told her that the nurse had insisted I wait for my doctor. She handled that news too easily. She was very cool and calm, as if she'd expected it.

The heck with the kidney stone, I was beginning to think like Oliver Stone. Was this a conspiracy? I was fit to be tied. I wanted my doctor to give me the A-OK sign and send me home. Instead, when he did return to my room, I got the somber news I had most dreaded hearing.

"I'm sorry to tell you this. There was no stone. Instead we found a tumor and it is cancerous. I don't know if we can help you or not at this point."

It felt like someone had poked me hard between the eyes with a baseball bat. The doctor said they would need to set up a schedule of intensive tests to fully assess my condition and to develop strategies for treatment. He said I should go home for the night because it would take a while to get the test appointments. But this is when I think God spoke to me in my affliction because I suddenly stopped playing the victim and started taking responsibility for my own treatment.

"I'm not going home today. I want to start the tests immediately so I know what I'm dealing with," I said. "I don't want to go home and face my three-year-old son without knowing how much more time I'll have with him."

Spirit of Hope

I did not want to face any more uncertainty. When the doctor told me that he couldn't get me into radiology on such short notice, I told him that he should try to pull a few strings, beginning with my personal physician and some contacts in the hospital administration. I may have had cancer, but I wasn't dead yet. In fact, I suddenly felt very much alive and determined to fight. Still, I needed to know the odds I was facing, and I wasn't about to check out of the hospital until I had a handle on that.

My determination must have impressed somebody because the next thing I knew, I was wheeled off for a CAT scan. Two hours later, Sonya and I met with a radiologist, my family doctor, and the urologist to review their findings. Initially, I felt like an exhibit brought to show-and-tell. A whole lot of smart folks were talking *about* me, but nobody was talking *to* me. They whispered, pointed, gestured, asked each other questions, and exchanged informed opinions. Then, finally, they talked to me—the dude with the problem.

They showed me photographs of a "normal" kidney—my good one. Then we got a look at a "diseased kidney"—mine too, unfortunately. The urologist didn't mess around. My only chance for survival was to have the diseased kidney removed. Then I could hope that my remaining kidney could handle the load. The surgeon was adamant that we needed to move quickly before the cancer spread if it hadn't already. I wasn't just hopeful—I was prayerful that we would stop the cancer and defeat the devil's plan.

My mental and emotional circuitry went on overload. I was about to lose it entirely when, praise Jesus, my spiritual circuitry saved the day. Before I could explode in anger and self-pity, God's spirit stepped in and took control of my mind, body, and soul. It was like an out-of-body experience. I had a sense of rising up out of myself and then looking down upon five people in the doctor's office as if observing them through a wide-angle lens from high above. The five people were the three doctors, Sonya, and me. I could hear myself talking, but the interesting thing was, I wasn't doing the talking. My mouth was moving and it sounded like my voice but, I'm telling you, there was a far greater power speaking through me.

I saw myself slam a fist on the doctor's desk and command their attention. Everyone jumped in their seats at the slam of my fist and the tone of my voice: "Listen to me! My God is going to use your abilities and knowledge to heal this body. Call whomever else you need to get the job done. Order up the MRI and the other tests and let's get them done so we can pick a date to operate and get this diseased kidney out of me!"

My out-of-body outburst seemed to be just what the doctor ordered. We had a plan. Everyone was on board. The mood became one of cooperation and compassion. I had the sensation of descending back down into my old self again. I had a new sense of self-control and confidence. I believe the Holy Spirit stepped in to take control of the situation. The Bible tells us that the righteous will stand for those who cannot stand for themselves. That day, I couldn't stand for myself. But God sent his Holy Spirit to stand for me, not only on that day but for many after.

This was my most difficult trial as a man and as a Christian. For the first time in my life, I was not up to the fight physically or mentally. I grew up with a strong sense of self-reliance. I'd long prided myself on being able to fight my own battles and to determine the course of my life. I'd done it as a boy, as a soldier, and in my career. But this was one fight that I couldn't go alone. I couldn't pick up a weapon and take on this scourge like an enemy combatant. This was a spiritual fight for my physical life, and it tested my relationship with Christ. The devil was trying to steal my joy, my faith, and my hope.

For weeks, I was entwined in fear, pain, panic, and self-pity. I lost perspective and turned inward to the point that my Lord Jesus Christ had to reach down, cut the bindings, and pull me out of myself so that I could see how low my faith was running. Only then, finally, did I realize how dire my situation had become. And then I humbly prayed for God to join me in battle.

I survived the operation, the removal of the cancerous kidney, and the challenges that ensued only because God sent his Holy Spirit to pull me out of my distress and to remind me of my faith. He gave me an emergency injection of hope that saved my life.

That's the most important thing I learned in this difficult walk with the Lord. Crisis separates the men from the boys, the women from the girls, and the truly faith-filled from the pretenders. It's easy to praise God when everything is going along smoothly and there is no stress or strain. But when the storms roll in and lightning paralyzes you in fear and panic, that's when you discover the depth of your faith. Theologians and scholars are all in agreement that crises will either draw you closer to God or drive you away from him. I can only thank God for his grace and his mercy, because he pulled me back in when my panic and fear nearly sent me running out of reach.

After my trial with kidney cancer and my deliverance by the Holy Spirit, I developed a deep interest in the book of Job. I'd read it before, but it had new meaning for me. Because of my own battle with cancer and all the suffering—both physical and mental—I went through, I wanted to know more about Job. I wanted an answer to his dilemma because I thought there would be an answer to mine. I wondered why God would allow any of this to happen to either of us! I knew I needed more understanding of this scripture. So when I began attending the seminary, I told my adviser I wanted to study the book of Job. Well, it didn't quite work out that way. I had to take a required class first. But later, one of my first electives was a class on the book of Job, which I loved. But did I find the answer I was looking for? No!

I lived much of my childhood in this Pittsburgh Plate Glass Company row house in Creighton, Pennsylvania, with my great-grandparents Walker and Susie Davis. Here I am at six years old. We had just returned from church.

If I had not already had religion, this is where I would have found it. I am a twenty-year-old paratrooper getting ready for a night jump at Fort Bragg, North Carolina, with the 82nd Airborne Division.

I came home on leave from the military to visit two great women in my life: my grand-mother Grace Bridges (in middle) and my mom, Dorothy Barnes. As you can tell, my mother was very independent and stately.

Former church choir singer Stevie Wonder has a musical range that includes stirring gospel soul songs like "As." His versatility and widespread appeal brought him to WNBC as the first rhythm and blues performer to be interviewed live on the radio. He is pictured with me; Ruben Rodriguez; an unidentified music director; and Mel Phillips, program director for WNBC.

The legendary "Walrus of Love" hangs out with Walt "Baby" Love. The late soul crooner Barry White visited me with record promoter Don Eason. Barry gained fame as a romantic R&B singer, but he grew up singing gospel with his mother in Galveston, Texas.

Even while broadcasting secular R&B music, I have shared my heavenly faith with Earth, Wind & Fire members Maurice White, Philip Bailey, and Verdine White.

Lionel Richie was still with the Commodores when we were pictured here, but he went on to a greater career as a solo artist, composer, and producer.

Grammy Award–winning songwriters and record producers Jimmy Jam Harris and Terry Lewis have worked with everyone from Janet Jackson to Gwen Stefani, Mariah Carey, Usher, and Jessica Simpson.

Eddie Murphy visited my *Countdown* show when he was starting his singing career.

The daughter of gospel great Cissy Houston, Whitney Houston began singing at the age of eleven in the junior gospel choir at the New Hope Baptist Church in Newark, New Jersey. She visited with me during a celebration of the #1 debut of her second album, *Whitney*, in 1987 at an Arista Records Promotions party.

Among performer, choreographer, and director Debbie Allen's many accomplishments is cowriting the gospel song "Stand Up" for the 1989 television movie *Polly*, which she also directed.

The New York Times hailed Tina Turner's "gospel style" rock and roll, and in 1974 she even cut a spiritual album entitled *The Gospel According to Ike and Tina*.

Grammy Award–winning artist Kirk Franklin and I at the 2004 Stellar Awards in Houston. Franklin, along with Kurt Carr, was kind enough to create the jingles for my *Gospel Traxx* radio show.

My long-time friend Yolanda Adams bridges the gap between R&B and gospel music. She is definitely a force to be reckoned with.

Well-known gospel singer and pastor, Bishop Paul S. Morton has been an inspiration in the development of my calling to ministry. He granted me the privilege of preaching at the Greater St. Stephen Full Gospel Baptist Church in New Orleans in 2002.

The Reverend Jesse Jackson, the founder of the RainbowPUSH Coalition, a religious and social progressive organization, invited me to a fund-raiser in Los Angeles in 2006.

Whether recording a track or preaching, Pastor Donnie McClurkin's mission is to report the good news of the gospel which I strive to do every week on my radio shows.

This high-energy, multitalented group Trin-I-Tee 5:7 have appeared numerous times on *Gospel Traxx* and at several of our fund-raiser events for lupus and cancer research.

I was a panelist at the 2003 annual Praise & Worship Conference, sponsored by the Gospel Heritage Foundation, that is designed to preserve the legacy of gospel music. Here I am with Bishop Eddie Long, who hosted a concert for the foundation at the New Birth Missionary Baptist Church near Atlanta.

Gospel icon Pastor Rance Allen has been recording music longer than I have been on the air!

At Pastor Charles Ellis III's Greater Grace Temple in Detroit, I thank Dr. Charles G. Hayes and Diane Williams for their performance during the Walt and Sonya Love Lupus and Cancer Research Foundation fund-raiser.

The professor who taught the class was very savvy. He said that three types of people took it: those who had to as a requirement, those who were just curious about Job, and those—like me—who had been through some traumatic incident and felt they could find the answer to their questions in his class. He informed all of us that we wouldn't find our answers there. It's not that simple, he said.

Yet I did learn that the Bible offers an outstanding example of the power of hope in the story of Job. It always restores and replenishes my optimism to read how Job held on to hope through all of his trials and was rewarded by God for his faith. When some think of Job's story, they think only of his trials and suffering, but his is really a story of hope, faith, trust in God, and divine deliverance. It is built upon his relationship with God *during* his suffering. After my own trial with kidney cancer and my deliverance by the Holy Spirit, I found it difficult but enlightening to do readings in the book of Job. So many of the things he said were similar to things that came out of my mouth when I was lost in my suffering: "Surely O God, you have worn me out. You have devastated my entire household."

Since my recovery from kidney cancer, I've given many public testimonials confessing that I did not live my faith as I should have during that battle. But, glory hallelujah and praise God: I had *enough*. Jesus said if you just have the faith of a mustard seed, you will be all right. I was extremely blessed physically and spiritually, and I acknowledge it every day in prayer. I often share with my radio audiences on all three of my music programs that God healed my body using medical science and intervention through early detection. He could have just made it disappear, but he chose to have me pick up my cross and go the distance through pain and suffering. God sent "physicians with healing hands" to do his work. I've been told that I had an advanced stage of cancer. My situation was grave. Yet God kept that cancer from spreading throughout my body.

After the diagnosis but prior to my surgery, I called Prophet Johnson to tell him what was going on. I asked him to pray for me. I figured that if anyone could get a prayer through on a direct line, it was Reverend Johnson. In that conversation, he ministered to me with kindness and understanding.

"Baby Love, don't you worry about a thing because it's going to be all right," he said. "I told you, God was going to give you a testimony that no one would be able to refute. I didn't know this was what it would be. Just remember this: God is able. And you belong to him."

His words touched me deeply, and they helped restore hope in my heart.

The Bible tells us that during a period of troubled times King David "encouraged himself in the Lord." That's exactly what I did when I finally returned to prayer. I encouraged myself in the Lord and asked him to grant me life by restoring my health and returning me to a sound state of mind.

During this trial, I listened to two favorite gospel songs over and over again: "Jesus, He's My King," by John P. Kee and the New Life Community Choir, and "Miracle Worker," by Rance Allen and the Rance Allen Group. The lyrics in those two songs helped me to put my faith into action by praising God. I am a living example, that Jesus is sure enough a miracle worker. When I need to ask God for his continued protection, I'll often listen to a gospel song by Fred Hammond and Radical for Christ. It's called "Jesus, Build a Fence," and it asks him to build a fence around us every day.

∾

Blessed is he who has regard for the weak; the LORD delivers him in times of trouble. The LORD will protect him and preserve his life; he will bless him in the land and not surrender him to the desire of his foes. The LORD will sustain him on his sickbed and restore him from his bed of illness.

—PSALM 41:1–3

∾

SEVEN

Stand Up for Jesus

GOSPEL OF LOVE:
Always defend and stand up for your faith

But the Lord said to Ananias, "Go! This man is my chosen instrument to carry my name before the Gentiles and their kings and before the people of Israel. I will show him how much he must suffer for my name."

—ACTS 9:15–16

As Christians we share the belief that the Lord Jesus Christ is our Savior. We also share the experience of dealing with scorn, shunning, ignorance, and suffering because of our Christian beliefs. Whether it is teen Christians mocked as "the God squad" or adult Christians subjected to more subtle prejudicial treatment, most true believers have felt discrimination of some sort. Suffering in God's name is a long Christian tradition. His Son, Jesus Christ, died for our sins and since that time, thousands and thousands have died and suffered in Jesus' name.

Saint Stephen is thought to be the first Christian martyr.

He was among the first seven deacons ordained to help the twelve apostles after Jesus died and was resurrected into heaven. So many people wanted to become Christians following the resurrection that the apostles needed help. They didn't know about outsourcing in those days, apparently. So instead, they ordained deacons to assist them by praying over them and placing their hands on their heads. Stephen, a Greek, was a charismatic and intelligent man "whose face was like the face of an angel." Stephen is described in glowing terms in the Bible as "a man full of faith and of the Holy Spirit."

First Martyr

Stephen's success drew the wrath of the Synagogue of the Freedmen. They sent people to argue with him in public and attack his Christian teachings, but Stephen was known as a very intelligent person and he was also an inspired debater. "They could not stand up against his wisdom or the Spirit by whom he spoke," according to Acts 6:10.

Frustrated, the leaders of the temple then persuaded spies to say that they'd heard Stephen tell lies about Moses and God. They had him arrested and brought to trial, just as they had done with Jesus.

Stephen did not back down, even though he knew this was a kangaroo court. He launched into a history of the rise of Christianity and near the end, he really let the Freedmen have it, calling them "stiff-necked people with uncircumcised hearts and ears," according to Acts 7:51. That did not sit well with his foes, of course. They were furious. Stephen realized that they were going to kill him. But still he did not back down. He looked up and said, "I see heaven open and the Son of Man standing at the right hand of God."

That drove the Freedmen to cover their ears and scream. They then dragged him outside the courtroom and to the edge of the town where they threw stones at him while a noted persecutor of Christians, Saul, looked on. We're told that Stephen prayed for his persecutors even as they stoned him to death, saying "Lord, do not hold this sin against them."

Converted Persecutor

Stephen died from the stoning, became a saint, and is recognized as the first Christian martyr. It's interesting that Saul, who witnessed the murder of Stephen, later became one of the most famous of all Christian converts and a martyr himself. Could God have heard Stephen's final prayer and responded by converting one of the most noted tormentors of Christians? Saul's miraculous conversion and new life as the Apostle Paul is generally considered to be second only to Jesus' death and resurrection in its importance to the creation of Christianity. Saul's conversion on the road to Damascus is one of the most powerful and dramatic events in the Bible. When I read of it in Acts 22 it always reminds me of the power of God, who converted this powerful enemy of Christianity into one of its greatest champions.

About noon as I came near Damascus, suddenly a bright light from heaven flashed around me. I fell to the ground and heard a voice say to me, "Saul! Saul! Why do you persecute me?"

"Who are you, Lord?" I asked.

"I am Jesus of Nazareth, whom you are persecuting," he replied. My companions saw the light, but they did not understand the voice of him who was speaking to me.

"What shall I do, Lord?" I asked.

"Get up," the Lord said, "and go into Damascus. There you will be told all that you have been assigned to do."

This new disciple stepped up and played a powerful role in the shaping of Christianity after Christ ascended into heaven. Paul, who was blinded, stoned, beaten, imprisoned, and ship-wrecked, suffered mightily for his faith. Yet he wrote more books of the New Testament than any other disciple. He was truly a Christian soldier.

Modern Persecution

Paul still serves as one of our greatest role models when we are challenged to stand up or fight for our faith. And those challenges are still faced by Christians all over the world. It is difficult to comprehend that thousands of years after Jesus walked this earth, there are still places where people of faith face death, torture, and torment because of their spiritual beliefs. Two religious rights groups—International Christian Concern and Christian Freedom International—have identified modern hot spots of persecution. The list is long and frightening to contemplate because it includes Afghanistan, Bangladesh, Belarus, Burma, China, Cuba, Egypt, Eritrea, Ethiopia, India, Indonesia, Iran, Iraq,

North Korea, Laos, Morocco, Myanmar, Nepal, Nigeria, Pakistan, Saudi Arabia, Sri Lanka, Sudan, Syria, United Arab Emirates, Vietnam, and Yemen among other areas. In Afghanistan alone, more than ten thousand converts face possible execution even as I write this. An Afghan man was given asylum in Italy in 2006 after an international outcry by Christian groups because of his arrest for "abandoning Islam," which carries the death penalty in his own country. Thousands of Burmese converts are also pleading for asylum in the United States.

Those of us who live in democratic nations that truly allow freedom of religion are blessed. But even in democratic countries, Christians are still confronted, challenged, and sometimes isolated because of their professed beliefs. The recent string of Baptist church burnings in Alabama may have been portrayed as a prank by misguided college students, but it is just the latest in a long series of periodic arson attacks on Christian churches in our own country.

Most Americans will never be stoned, beaten, or imprisoned like Paul. Still, we must be vigilant and ready to respond to religious persecution. And always we must stand up and be true to our Christian beliefs even when it is not convenient or safe or "cool" to profess that we love God and Jesus Christ as our Savior.

Silenced

Like many Christians, I've experienced different shades of discrimination, some subtle, others more overt. Of course, as a black man, I might be considered a double-dipper in the discrimination department. And though the entertainment indus-

try is often portrayed as the most liberal of arenas, radio broadcasting has not always been a comfortable place to be a strong
Christian. At times, especially in the early days of my career, I
found my coworkers and superiors were inhospitable to people
of faith. That is why you can hear *The Countdown with Walt "Baby"*
Love syndicated rhythm and blues radio show in scores of nations around the world—in remote corners of Africa, Europe,
Asia, and the Caribbean—but you cannot hear it in Chicago.

That show is not heard in the third-largest radio market in
the United States because approximately a decade ago I defied
the decree of a single program director by mentioning the
name Jesus Christ on the air. And when he demanded that I
stop doing that, I told him that as a true believer, I could never
deny my faith or hide the truth of my Christianity. I told him
that expressing my faith was just a natural part of who I am
and that I could not deny it. Jesus is with me every minute of
every day and I have to express that. To do so would be to deny
Jesus and I cannot and will not do that.

Little did I know then that standing up for my faith in Jesus
in the broadcast booth would bring the damnation of a powerful program director down upon me. Because I stood up to
that nonbeliever and stood up for my faith, my contract with
that station was not renewed. My syndicated R&B show is still
not heard on Chicago radio to this day, even though it is the
longest-running black syndicated show in history! Now, there
are certainly far worse things that have happened to Christians
who stood up for their faith, but this is an example of how
nonbelievers attempt to make us pay if we don't join the secular world, if we insist on acknowledging that Jesus Christ is in
our hearts and minds at all times.

One of the many ironies of the "blackballing" of my *Countdown* show on this Chicago radio station because of my Christian outspokenness is that it targets the African American community. Last I checked, 88 percent of African Americans in this country are followers of Christianity. Most blacks are not Buddhists, Hindus, Muslims, Hare Krishnas, or atheists. It is also strange that I was taken off that station because I occasionally mentioned the name of Jesus on my broadcasts aimed at African Americans. If there is any group of people who invoke Jesus' name in daily conversation more than black folks, I've yet to meet them.

My trials with this Chicago radio station began after this program director said to me out of the blue one day: "Do you have to mention that word on your show? I don't like it."

Naturally, I asked him what word he was referring to.

"Jesus!" he said.

I then told this "brother-man" the realities of my Christian life. "To me, this 'word' that offends you is precious. It is the name of my Lord and Savior Jesus the Christ," I said.

He was not impressed. He told me that he respected that I believed in God but that he did not.

It was the first and only time in my life I've heard a black person claim to be an atheist. I was shocked, angry, and horrified. After all, this person was in charge of deciding what black folks in the city of Chicago got to hear or didn't get to hear on a very powerful radio station. Radio stations use public airwaves to make a profit, but only with government permission. Their broadcast licenses require radio stations to serve the interests of the community. Given that the black community is predominantly Christian, I don't believe this atheist was capable of serving their interests. There have been instances when black listeners have revolted against radio stations that did not serve their needs, wants, and desires, and rightly so. Radio stations should pay close attention, and their programming should reflect the public's interest. I've always encouraged black community and church leaders to monitor their radio stations. But I'm afraid that since the Telecommunications Bill of 1996 allowed consolidation of the broadcast industry, the corporate giants that control the airwaves have tuned out their listeners and focused on profits.

Looking back, the irony is wicked. Today, Howard Stern and other shock jocks make millions and millions of dollars spewing bile and decadence on their huge syndicated shows, yet I was being banned from one of the largest broadcasting markets in the country because I promoted the word of God! Isn't there an FCC rule somewhere that says God's message should get equal time with Satan's? To put things in perspective, it wasn't like I was preaching on the air or trying to recruit or rehabilitate sinners. It was much more benign than that.

I simply and naturally would drop the name of Jesus now and then during the *Countdown* show. It wasn't a planned thing where I sat down and worked out a schedule: *Let's see, I've got to say, 'Jesus loves you' every hour on the hour, so right after this funky Earth, Wind and Fire hit I'll drop it in. Praise Jesus!* It was far more casual than that. In doing the R&B show I might come on after a particularly touching ballad and say something along the lines of "When things go wrong, don't turn to the bottle or give in to despair, remember that God loves you and ask Jesus to help you and he will."

That was it. No Bible thumping. No hellfire and brimstone. Just a simple encouraging statement in the name of

God. I often received messages from listeners all over the world telling me they appreciated those brief Christian asides. They expressed their thanks in letters, postcards, email, and faxes then and even to this day. In fact, just before this confrontation of faith in Chicago, the vice president and general manager of the radio station sent me a complimentary note regarding one of my supposedly offensive outbursts of Christian expression. In his note, he told me how much he and his mother, who was visiting in Chicago one weekend, enjoyed my comments encouraging people to look to the Lord during my broadcast.

I keep that complimentary note and also the original letter I received from the program director telling me to stop talking about and mentioning Jesus' name. It reminds me that I should never take for granted either my faith or my freedom to express it. When Jesus preached the Sermon on the Mount and gave the Beatitudes to the disciples, Christians were presented with a profound moment in the history of their faith. The Beatitudes can be found in Matthew 5:1–14. In verses 10–12, Jesus says, "Blessed are those who are persecuted because of righteousness, for theirs is the kingdom of heaven."

He goes on to say that we are also blessed when people insult us, persecute us, and say false things about us. Instead of running and hiding or lashing out against our persecutors, we should "rejoice and be glad because great is your reward in heaven." You gotta like that, don't you? Our reward is in heaven! Praise the Lord. Now that doesn't mean that we should walk around with chips on our shoulders or with victim mentalities. I'm personally not the least bit interested in being persecuted for my faith. I don't need the stress and I'm sure you don't either. It's natural to prefer peace and quiet and harmony. But when someone does discriminate against you, mock you, or razz you for expressing your Christian beliefs, it's nice to consider that you are on God's own heavenly rewards program— and it sure beats the one at American Express!

Power in Weakness

When Jesus delivered the message that our rewards await us in heaven, he was providing us with a source of strength so that we could endure the challenges to our faith. The Apostle Paul tells us that he had "a thorn" in his flesh and that three times he asked the Lord to take it away from him. The Lord did not do it. Instead he told him, "My grace is sufficient for you, for my power is made perfect in weakness" (2 Corinthians 12:9a). Paul responds in verses 9b–10:

> *"Therefore, I will boast all the more gladly about my weaknesses, so that Christ's power may rest on me. That is why, for Christ's sake, I delight in weaknesses, in insults, in hardships, in persecutions, in difficulties. For when I am weak, then I am strong."*

God is our strength and our salvation. Paul is telling us that it is okay if we sometimes feel weak and vulnerable, because Jesus is there to support us and to give us the power to keep on keeping on. The Bible doesn't tell us what Paul's thorn in the flesh was. Maybe it was his own self-doubt. Whatever it was, it kept him humble and dependent on God. He realized that the only true source of strength comes from God. We need to remember that too. We should never be afraid, because our weak-

nesses and flaws are imperfections that remind us of God's perfect love and its value in our lives. To become powerful Christians we must learn to continually call on God, while also
giving him the glory in our lives. I don't know about you, but
I'm always telling folks about something God did in my life to
make my path clear. I've now learned that every time I succeed
at something monumental, it's only because of God and his
grace and mercy.

Still, back when my program director was pushing my buttons, it really rocked my boat. I had some very righteous indig-
nation going and only God could give me peace. I did
everything I could personally and professionally to fight him
and his edict against expressing my Christian beliefs on the air
during my rhythm and blues show. The vice president and general manager even weighed in at one point and suggested that
we work out an amicable solution. The GM was very polite
and diplomatic. He told me that he would like to see the two
of us black men work this thing out before it got ugly for all
concerned. He stressed that we should view each other as
brothers. I agreed, at least in theory. He instructed me to call
the program director, which I respectfully did.

This Is a Test

Now, let me step up here and confess an imperfection, or two,
or three. At that point in my walk with the Lord, I was a little
shaky. I wasn't a mature Christian. I didn't have the depth of
understanding that I do today—and I've still got a ways to go.
I understand now that I was being tested back then, just as true
Christians are tested every day in many ways. The Lord had

handed out a pop quiz to see if I'd learned to love my enemies—one of his most important teachings.

When Jesus laid down the guidelines for his disciples to
follow once he departed this earth, he told them to "love and
pray for their enemies." I'm sure all of the apostles must have
looked at each other and wondered how they ever would have
lived up to that one. After all, they were expected to go out and
teach the word of God in a largely hostile environment, and
Jesus was in effect telling them, "Oh, by the way, if someone
attacks you for doing the work I've assigned, you should simply
love and pray for them." Jesus expected the apostles to understand that if they'd just shower love on their enemies, he'd take
care of the retribution stuff down the road. God would admin-
ister the justice. The disciples and the rest of us mere mortals
are supposed to let the man upstairs take care of that. The disciples were warned that they would be persecuted and rejected
by their enemies, but Jesus assured them that God would judge
the persecutors when the time came. He lays it out plain and
simple in Luke 6:27–36: "But I tell you who hear me: Love
your enemies, do good to those who hate you, bless those who
curse you, pray for those who mistreat you."

Jesus knew that his disciples would be scorned and attacked
for their Christian beliefs, so he gave them this powerful
weapon—love. If you just love your enemies, your rewards will
come. He wanted his disciples to look for the good in everyone.

Love Your Enemies

I've got to confess: I'm still not the best at living this important
Christian principle. I'm afraid I'm still a work in progress on

that one. I'm still a long way from giving Saddam Hussein or the Ku Klux Klan a hug. But, seriously, no one who witnessed Nelson Mandela's victory over apartheid can deny the power of *loving your enemies.* Mandela won over his own jailers by refusing to hate them. He made peace with his enemies and worked with them until they became partners in bringing down apartheid. Mandela once told an interviewer, "Our talking with the enemy was a domination of the brain over emotion, without which our country would have turned into rivers of blood." Such wisdom! Black people have a rich history of powerful, intelligent, wise, and successful leaders, and Mandela is certainly near the top of that list.

Gandhi, who served as a role model to Tutu, Mandela, and Dr. Martin Luther King Jr., once said, "An eye for an eye leaves the world blind." Jesus didn't ask his followers to simply treat their enemies decently; he demanded that Christians love their enemies as they loved themselves. There is nothing wishy-washy about that. We are supposed to look into the eyes of those who have wronged us and acknowledge that they too are children of God. As Tutu has noted also: "Jesus did not demand that we should be merely good. No, he challenged us to be perfect, to seek to emulate the perfection of God, who makes the sun shine on good and bad alike. We are exhorted to forgive one another even as God in Christ forgave us; we are in the forgiving business whether we like it or not. And we can do this only through God's grace. It is ultimately God at work in us to make us to be like God."

Another black leader who lived this Christian philosophy even before Mandela and Tutu was Richard Allen, the founder of the African Methodist Church. He was born into slavery in

1760 in Philadelphia and became one of the first African Americans emancipated during the Revolutionary War era, as well as the first black ordained and licensed to preach in America. He and another black preacher, Absalom Jones, helped form the Free African Society, which helped many blacks escape slavery and its bonds.

Since he identified so strongly with his racial heritage, Allen declined to join the mainstream white Methodist or other congregations, some of which practiced racism in various forms. He did not abandon his faith, and he was known for working with white leaders rather than fighting against them, whenever possible. Allen created the Bethel African Methodist Episcopal Church in 1794 because he did not want blacks of faith to be dominated by the white-controlled power structure of other churches. By 1813, his church had 1,272 members even though it had sanctions against drinking, gambling, and infidelity. In 1816, the A.M.E. Church was recognized as an independent denomination. Allen and his followers fought slavery laws and the slave trade, demanding a repeal of the Fugitive Slave Act of 1793 that allowed slave owners to seize blacks without a warrant. Allen was himself taken temporarily as a fugitive slave in 1806, which led to his initial support for the American Colonization Society, a mostly white group that sought the resettlement of free blacks in Africa. But Allen quickly saw the folly of that plan. He briefly favored a similar plan for blacks in Hawaii (I like that idea too), but eventually he decided that blacks should stay put in "this land which we have watered with our tears and our blood . . ."

Richard Allen, like Tutu and Mandela, followed the teachings of Matthew 5:43–45, which urge us to put aside bitter-

ness and to "Love your enemies and pray for those who persecute you, that you may be sons of your Father in heaven."
Matthew notes that God's sun rises on both the evil and the
good, and that his rain falls on both the righteous and unright-
eous. The message is that we get no special privileges as believers. We have to love God, serve God, believe God, and follow
God in the good times and bad if we really are his disciples.

Living God's Teachings

As an African American Christian, I have always walked a difficult path in my chosen field of broadcasting. The connections
made with listeners are rich treasures that make each day a
blessing. But to get to those rewards, I've had to fight off petty
jealousy, treachery, and betrayal time and time again. Every
black person has stories of racial prejudice. Every Christian has
the challenge of living the faith amidst corruption, temptation,
and derision. I've had all of that and more, and because of
those challenges I have struggled with loving my enemies.

I truly believe that solid Christians can master this one, but
it takes strong faith, a lot of prayer, and time. Lord knows, I've
put in a lot of time on this one myself. The broadcasting industry can be as cutthroat as any field out there. That is true
even today because the financial stakes are so high and the
competition is so intense for the dwindling number of on-air
jobs and management positions. During my thirty-plus years in
the industry, things have always been rough and tumble. Having skin the color of coffee with cream doesn't make it any easier. In fact, it is even tougher for African Americans today than
it was when I was getting started. Consolidation, new technolo-

gies, and automation have cut the number of positions so competition for jobs is more intense than ever in this new millennium. In the wake of the civil rights movement, there was at least a widespread sense that society had an obligation to level the playing field for African Americans who'd been discriminated against so long. That sense now seems to have disappeared, for the most part.

The early days were probably harder on me psychologically because my hide had not been thickened by the constant chafing against racism, discrimination, ignorance, and antireligious sentiments found in the broadcast realm. I got hurt, often by people who didn't know me well. But that's life. We all get hurt and we either learn to take our lumps or we give up and go home. There were points when bitterness began to take hold, but usually my faith saved me. At one point I turned mean, like a dog that'd been mistreated by a bad owner. Rather than put up with more abuse in the entertainment industry, I lashed out at the predatory types who circle like wolves looking for the weak to stumble. That's when I realized that I had to get my butt back in church and wrap myself up in Jesus.

I wasn't well versed in those Christian principles at the time, but I did try to reconcile with the black program director whose atheist beliefs led him to ban my occasional references to my faith on the rhythm and blues show. But when I spoke to him, he rebuffed my attempts to work things out. He said that he only took my call at the request of the general manager, who was trying to play peacemaker. He still demanded that I not mention Jesus or other Christian beliefs during my *Countdown* show. He told me I should leave "that kind of stuff" for my gospel music broadcasts instead. So he held his ground. *Count-*

down would lose its spot of many years on Sunday night as long as I insisted on expressing my Christianity on the air. There was no offer of a compromise.

The really odd thing in all this is that I had helped this program director get a job earlier in his career when an employer called me for a reference. I'd thought we were friends. But, as you probably have experienced, sometimes people resent it when you help them because it makes them look needy. That may have been why this guy was playing the power game with me at this point. And there was no doubt: he held the controls at this radio station. So I had to make a choice. And I chose not to walk away from my faith and bow to his demand. Instead, I walked away from doing my *Countdown* show at his station.

Pearls to Pigs

Whenever I reflect upon that incident today, I think of Matthew 7:6, which offers this sage advice: "Do not give dogs what is sacred; do not throw your pearls to pigs. If you do, they may trample them under their feet, and then turn and tear you to pieces." Had I been a little wiser in my understanding of the Bible and my faith back then, I might have simply walked away from this fight entirely. I would have saved my pronunciations of faith for my gospel show and prayed for the program director's troubled soul. At the time, I lacked the wisdom that comes with the gift of the Holy Spirit. In John 16, Jesus tells us of "the Counselor" who will be sent by God the Father. We are told that when this Spirit of truth comes, he will guide us into all truth. Jesus says that the Spirit will take from what is his and make it known to us.

The Bible also tells us that the Holy Spirit investigates and examines matters for us and then shows us what it is we should know and what we should or should not do about a situation. In John 15:26, we're told that the Holy Spirit will guide us into all truth. Jesus called the Holy Spirit "the Counselor" and said he would send the Holy Spirit to counsel the disciples when they needed help after his death. The Holy Spirit is sometimes called "the Spirit of Truth." He ministers to the head and to the heart. The Holy Spirit guides us. We need to listen to his voice, which is that "little voice" in our heads trying to keep us on the straight and narrow. The Holy Spirit is a gift from God. If you believe in Christ Jesus, the Holy Spirit is "given" to you and the only thing you can do is accept this gift.

Unfortunately, I was still maturing in my Christian faith. I lacked wisdom, and I was at an age where I felt I had to assert myself and show strength rather than seek understanding. What I didn't realize was that it takes more strength to love your enemies than it does to hate them or to fight back. In Joshua 1:1–11, God tells Joshua three times to "be strong and courageous." He was urging Joshua to be strong in his faith and commitment to serve God's purposes. We must be committed to what God wants, and he wants us to forgive and love our enemies even as we stand up for our faith. We have to be courageous enough to trust God with our lives. That is the bottom line.

Putting It on the Line

We have to be willing to put it all out there for God and then to be ready to accept the consequences. It's often difficult for immature Christians—and we are all learning and growing every day—to understand that suffering, sacrifice, and struggle are part of the process. We have to trust that if we are strong in our faith and in following God's guidance, he will take care of the small stuff and the big stuff too. God wants us to be obedient too. Joshua is again our example. Out of twelve spies, only Joshua and Caleb believed with total trust that God would help them conquer the promised land of Canaan. You and I have to believe that God will help us conquer our fears and make it to the promised land.

God has promised us that. We must overcome our emotions and abandon the concepts of retribution so that we can practice forgiveness and healing. In Joshua 1, verse 6, we're told "Be strong and courageous because you will lead these people to inherit the land I swore to their forefathers to give them." Verse 7 repeats that important point but adds emphasis: "Be strong and *very* courageous. Be careful to obey all the law my servant Moses gave you; do not turn from it to the right or to the left, that you may be successful wherever you go."

If we hope to be successful, we've got to be *very* courageous. We've got to be passionate, not wishy-washy or wimpy Christians. We can't be lukewarm about our faith. We can't be punks. We have to be prepared to suffer the consequences of standing up for Christ and that is what I did. I never compromised. I never gave up speaking about Christ. This atheist I was dealing with professed to hate Christians and their beliefs, so I should have been modeling for him the example that God wants us to set. But I was not supposed to compromise. The secular world will only come to understand us if we fight back with love and forgiveness. We've got to have a Joshua kind of faith and strength and courage to do God's work in a secularized society.

Back in Chicago, I was a little confused about all that, but that's what life is all about. We live and we learn. I'd been raised to stand up for my belief, even if I had to take a beating. In this case, it was a financial beating. As a last resort, I reached out to the Chicago headquarters of this station's broadcasting company. I spoke with the president and CEO. He was extremely cordial and patient as I explained the situation. Later, he gave me even more of an audience in a face-to-face meeting. The broadcast CEO came to my office in Los Angeles while in town for business. I showed him copies of the program director's letter ordering me to "knock off the Jesus stuff." Then I presented him with the encouraging note from the station manager about the impact of my Christian comments on the air for him and his mother. The CEO graciously promised to look into my complaint, but he cautioned that he would not interfere with his management team's decision. He said it sounded like a personal issue between me and the program director. I agreed. I compared it to black-on-black crime in which people of the same race prey upon each other when they should be supporting each other. In this case, however, two black men had risen above the street and into corporate America and we should have risen above our differences too.

Instead, there was a street mentality at play here. You could almost hear it in the background tones of jealousy. The program director was playing the role of a street gang member claiming his turf. His attitude said: "Who do you think you are, nigger? This is my territory and you will play by my rules—or else."

I had to deal with the "or else." There we were, two black men struggling to succeed in a white man's world and we were at each other's throats. To me, that's not just misguided. It's what the book of Proverbs calls "a fool and his folly." It's also a shame. God brought my people out of Egypt and into the promised land. And what did we do? We fought among ourselves. In the end, over many years, this rivalry played out. The program director eventually left that job. And today my voice is heard in Chicago, though not on that station. My syndicated show is on a competing station that carries not the rhythm and blues show but my *Gospel Traxx* show.

Hold On to Faith

As a believer and as a person of color, I have to hold on to my faith and stand for what I believe. Each of us has to fight to build a relationship with God. We must commit to hold on. After all I have experienced and gone through, I can't let go! In the little-known Old Testament Book of Nahum, there is something that speaks to me. Nahum 1:7 says: "The LORD is good, a refuge in times of trouble. He cares for those who trust in him."

The Amplified Bible's translation of the same scripture, Nahum 1:7: says: "The Lord is good, a Strength and Stronghold in the day of trouble; He knows those who take refuge and trust in Him"

God is my strength and stronghold at all times and certainly when I was going through this hellacious trying time, he was there for me. I still had one foot in the world and one foot in God's kingdom. I wanted to believe that, because I was standing for what was right and good for humanity while also doing what was right for my business and our affiliate radio station's business. We need to reach the largest possible audience in each market. When we lost that Chicago station, it shook me up and rattled my business temporarily.

Once again, Prophet Johnson with his wisdom came to the rescue. He said to me, "I know you're disappointed and upset. I also know that when you came over to this side of the church world that you thought everything would be different and you wouldn't have to be concerned about things. Let it go. God will give you something else down the road in some other place. You can't fight all your battles like you used to. You have to let go and let God!"

Finally, I did. And God took care of business—and me, his humbled child.

The Williams Brothers of Quartet Gospel fame sing a song that really speaks to my spirit about making it through difficult times. It's called "I'm Still Here." It could be my theme song, and I'm sure a lot of other folks feel that way, too. We face many challenges and trials and tribulations, but it's a good day when at the end of it we can sing "I'm Still Here."

꒰

In fact, everyone who wants to live a godly life in Christ Jesus will be persecuted, while evil men and imposters will go from bad to worse, deceiving and being deceived.

—2 TIMOTHY 3:12–13

꒰

EIGHT

Know the Power of God's Forgiveness

GOSPEL OF LOVE:
Forgive others, but most of all, yourself

If we claim to be without sin, we deceive ourselves
and the truth is not in us. If we confess our sins, he
is faithful and just and will forgive us our sins and
purify us from all unrighteousness.

—1 JOHN 1:8–9

I had a severe anxiety attack in the fall of 1991 and my medical doctor suggested that I talk with a psychiatrist to "catch this thing before it becomes a real problem." My anxiety was triggered by an accident at home. It was one of those all-too-common mental lapses during a routine activity that impacts you for years to come. It was a simple goof, but I nearly cut off one of the fingers on my left hand. I really, really hate to admit it, but it happened because I didn't listen to my wife's advice. (Ouch, it still hurts to admit that!)

We were in the kitchen talking. I'd just come home from

work. As we talked, I noticed this exquisite long-stemmed crystal goblet sitting on the counter next to the sink. It belonged to a set of crystal we'd received as a wedding gift. I asked Sonya why it was sitting out. She told me it was cracked.

"Don't touch it, I'm going to throw it away before it breaks completely," she said.

Naturally, as a stubborn male my response was to do exactly what my wife had cautioned me not to do. I picked up the crystal goblet. I barely got it off the counter when I heard a muffled "crack!" and felt a sharp pain in my left hand just as an amazingly powerful stream of blood shot out of it and hit me right between the eyes!

I wasn't walking with the Lord as I should have been then. I was in one of my "backslides" due to too much focus on work and not enough time spent practicing my faith. We had a baby on the way and I was a little panicked about providing for my family. Due to my backsliding—I've been setting this up, in case you had not noticed—I didn't asked for God's mercy when I cut my finger and blood shot out of my hand. Instead, I yelled an expletive that no doubt shook the heavens. God still responded with mercy. He kept my mind clear enough that I remembered some of my military training in first aid. I immediately applied pressure to the open wound. It was a good thing I did because my poor finger was cut to the bone. I'd also severed an artery and cut a tendon. I'd reacted quickly, but there was already blood everywhere. It looked like our kitchen had been decorated by Stephen King.

Sonya was screaming, demanding to know what I'd done. I asked her to dial 911 for me. Then I told her to get out because I didn't want her to see all that blood. Because of her pregnancy, I didn't want her getting too upset or too panicked. I needed reinforcements, preferably with stretchers and painkillers on the truck. I'd sealed off the wound fairly well with my undamaged hand, but I realized that I needed to fashion a tourniquet of some kind so the blood flow would be shut off even if I passed out from shock. So I released the finger just long enough to grab my belt and pull it off. I had to hold one end in my mouth to keep it tightly wrapped around my left arm. I was a happy camper when the paramedics and three firemen walked in the house—even if the firemen seemed like more cavalry than I needed.

Once they saw that I'd stopped the bleeding on my own, they teased that they might have to arrest me for causing the "pretty young lady outside" to be so upset. Then the paramedics took a look at what the goblet had done to my finger and decided that it was a pretty serious injury. The initial shock was wearing off and I was feeling some intense pains shooting through my hand and arm.

To distract myself, I used another method from my army survival training, I kept repeating the paratroopers' mantra: *Airborne . . . all the way, baby! Airborne . . . all the way, baby! Airborne . . . all the way, baby!* Now that I'm saved and have more in-depth knowledge about the Bible, I know that the power of life and death are in the tongue. We speak to confess our sins and accept Jesus as our Lord and Savior. One must speak life and we must speak life at all times. To veteran paratroopers the phrase "Airborne all the way" expresses exuberant life, pride, courage, excellence, endurance, focus, teamwork, love, and strength. We used it to take our minds off fatigue, fear, and our own aches and pains during training. In my kitchen crisis, it helped me keep from screaming because of the stabbing pains in my limb. The paramedics thought it was hilarious, of course. They laughed as they stopped the bleeding, cleaned my wound, and applied a more professional dressing. Then we discussed which hospital might have a hand surgeon on duty to tend to my injury. They were a good and caring team of professionals. One even complimented me on my efforts at first aid, learned in the 82nd Airborne. He also noted the cross around my neck and said: "God has a way of taking care of his own."

His comment struck me because I hadn't been thinking much about God or my faith much during my crystal cut incident. The paramedic reminded me that I should have been honoring and thanking God for enabling me to remember my first aid training so that I hadn't bled to death, passed out, or gone into shock. I had more time to think about his comments and the role God played in my life during my treatment and recuperation from that accident. It dawned on me that I'd gotten out of step with God. He was not as big a part of my daily existence as I wanted him to be. In a sense, I had deserted him, but he hadn't left me alone. He was right there in the midst of my bloody mess, to be sure.

When we arrived at the hospital, the nurses called for their hand specialist, who was not on duty that night. So the doctor in the emergency room stitched me up after trying to deaden the finger. It didn't work. I felt a stab of pain every time my heart beat. I didn't try to hide it either. My finger was an ugly mess and that didn't help my attitude. It looked like a raw piece of meat that had been sliced by a butcher's meat cleaver. The emergency room doctor even remarked that the crystal had made a nice clean cut. It was a good thing since I cut my hand on a Friday night and didn't see a hand surgeon until early Monday morning. (Note to self: Conduct all future mutilations during regular hospital hours!)

The hand surgeon examined my wound and the X-rays of it and ruled that I needed to go under his knife to fix the damage done by the broken crystal. My finger would not have full range of motion unless he could go in and repair it, he said. Unfortunately, I let him operate on my hand but was left wondering whether he had botched the job. Several weeks of physical therapy produced little progress. The injured finger didn't bend. I couldn't type or grip a golf club. So I sought a second opinion from another surgeon recommended as the best in the Los Angeles area. This hand specialist, who practiced at UCLA Medical Center in Westwood, decided he could improve my finger's range of motion if I was willing to undergo another surgery. I was impressed with this more personable doctor, who seemed to be a caring person, so I agreed to have him schedule the surgery.

And then I went home and came apart at the seams.

I've dealt with kidney cancer so this crystal cut finger seems, at least in retrospect, to have been a fairly middlin' crisis in the span of my life. Yet in the midst of it, the devil came knocking on my door and caused me no end of serious grief. My finger, it seemed, was just the first nick of his demonic blade. Satan then attacked my mind and set off a downward spiral of the spirit. My descent into darkness began a few nights after I saw the second surgeon. I returned home after putting in fourteen hours on my "regular day job" as the urban radio and music editor at *Radio & Records* weekly newspaper, where I wrote a column for more than twenty years. Sonya and I had returned to the scene of the crime—our kitchen—and I was telling her about my frustrating day, trying to type on my computer with a frozen digit on my left hand, and dealing with other routine problems that suddenly seemed overwhelming to me.

To her credit as a good Christian, Sonya kept telling me to calm down and to trust in God because he would work it out for me. But my sensory circuits were on overload for reasons I could not fathom. Suddenly, I started perspiring heavily. My heart began beating as frenetically as a Buddy Rich drum solo. I felt like my brain was boiling. I announced to Sonya that I had to get out of the house, that the heat was making it hard to breathe. It was a very cool winter night in Southern California, but stepping outside didn't help. That's when it dawned on me that I was having some sort of physical or mental breakdown.

Later, I learned that my rush to get outside was a classic fight-or-flight response to the excessive amounts of adrenaline that were flowing through my body. In essence, I'd been right. My brain was boiling as the result of an anxiety attack. My medical emergency and the complications that followed had apparently been the straw that broke the back of my over-loaded psyche. Certainly there were millions of people out there dealing with much heavier emotional loads than what was burdening me. Still, I broke down.

I found myself sitting on the curb in front of our house with my poor pregnant wife trying to soothe me and coach me back inside so the neighbors wouldn't call the guys in white coats. I'm sure the devil was digging it. He had me on the ropes with a sucker punch. I never saw it coming. But if I'd been a lit-tle more tuned in to the Bible, I might have had a clue—or two or three—from the wizard of Uz—Job.

After all, Job too was a man of considerable achievement.

We're told that he was a "blameless and upright" God-fearing man who shunned evil. A resident of Uz (believed to be somewhere east of Palestine), he had seven sons, three daughters, seven thousand sheep, three thousand camels, five hundred yoke of oxen, five hundred donkeys, and a huge staff of servants. And one day, out of the blue, Satan dropped in and started messing with Job just like he was messing with me.

As we're told in Job 1:7–8: The LORD said to Satan, "Where have you come from?" Satan answered the LORD, "From roaming through the earth and going back and forth in it." Then the LORD said to Satan, "Have you considered my servant Job?"

Satan more or less challenged God, claiming that Job was a good and faithful servant only because he'd been blessed and had such a good life.

"But stretch out your hand and strike everything he has, and he will surely curse you to your face," Satan tells God in Job 1:11.

The Lord then accepted that challenge and, for me, his response now seems more than a little eerie: "The LORD said to Satan, 'Very well, then, everything he has is in your hands, but on the man himself do not lay a finger.'"

Satan then set off the trial of Job, just as he seemed to have set off mine, wreaking havoc in his life. But Job stayed true to his faith in God throughout his trials, and Satan lost the bet. "Naked I came from my mother's womb, and naked I will depart," Job says. "The LORD gave and the LORD has taken away; may the name of the LORD be praised" (Job 1:21).

Sonya must have sensed that the devil was testing me, too, because when I wouldn't listen to reason on that curb, she turned to prayer. She had called my doctor and then tried to get

me to come into the house and talk to him on the phone, but I refused. I was obsessed with the notion that there was something dangerous in the house. Sonya then started praying for some divine intervention and the Holy Spirit answered her calls. It was like Jesus stepped in and told the devil to back off. My craziness subsided. I stopped sweating. My heart slowed down. My senses returned to the point that I, too, began to pray.

It was scary. No, it was torture. I'd lost control of my mental faculties. It was like I'd fallen into some evil Edgar Allan Poe scenario. My great-grandmother Susie used to tell me that the devil can't hurt you, but he can make you hurt yourself. Sonya was frightened too. She'd put out a call for help and as a result we received a phone call from a psychiatrist referred by our family doctor. He offered to set up an appointment and he prescribed medication to tide me over. I didn't like the idea of taking drugs to ease my mind. I preferred to pray for God's help on such matters. Still, I got the medications and took them because I was scared about what had happened to me. A few days later, I met with my "analyst," as they are called here in Southern California. I guess that officially made me a member of the Hollywood crowd.

I put my trust in God; psychiatry was a whole new matter. Yet, as it turned out, I kept seeing this psychiatrist for a number of years and he helped me work out some issues that apparently contributed to my frightening anxiety attack. It is interesting, though, because one of the basic things I learned from the analyst and his therapy was that I needed to more closely follow God's lessons on forgiveness.

My therapy brought to the surface a lot of anger that had been built up over the years. It was affecting my mental and

physical health far more than I realized, according to my analyst. In our talks, I brought up many instances in which I felt discriminated against or mistreated by whites with power over my career in the broadcasting field. We talked about other incidents from my childhood in Creighton. It dawned on me that things I'd let slide or "gotten over" had not gone away. They were stacked up somewhere in my mind like toxic waste and they were eating away at my mental health to the point that they'd eventually impacted my physical health too. The anxiety attack was just the first major indication that I was being poisoned from within.

The psychiatrist said I had "anger management" problems to work on. At first that made no sense to me. I told him I'd dealt with the issues and put them behind me. I really did think that things were not affecting me. I'd been taught since childhood to move on. "Don't cry about it. Suck it up and keep going. Be a man." Still, the more we talked in those therapy sessions, the more I had to admit that I was carrying a lot of negative baggage, including hurt feelings, betrayals, issues of self-esteem, feelings of victimization, racial resentment, and guilt over my inability to be as good a Christian as I aspired to be.

One of the major incidents that surfaced was one in which I had been recommended for a high-level management position at a record company. I didn't get the job and later I was told by acquaintances that those who'd interviewed me felt that I was the most qualified but I was "too straight" and "too honest" to run the black music division of that record label. It would have been a lucrative, prestigious, and exciting position, so I was definitely upset at the time when I didn't get it. Obviously, the record company's top executives thought I was naïve. An inno-

cent among the wolves. That made me angry. For a brief stretch, I wanted to rip into the world, but I thought I got over it. Apparently, I didn't.

To end the dark period that followed my rejection for that job, I'd leaned on my faith in God. I prayed and I asked for his understanding and blessing. I thought I got it all together. Instead, the anger was just stored on a back burner of my mind where it simmered and stewed into a toxic brew. I had relied on my faith to carry me through the pain and anger, which was fine. But I was misguided in my approach. I was praying for strength and the power to move on, but what I really needed was the healing power of forgiveness on the mind, body, and the spirit.

As a Christian, I'd accepted that forgiveness has spiritual power, even though I may have been negligent in practicing it myself. But I was not aware that even scientists, physicians, psychologists, and brain researchers have come to accept the mental and physical healing that forgiveness can bring. Studies have shown that forgiveness can reduce blood pressure and stress hormone levels, particularly among low-income black folks. Hallelujah for that! It can also lessen pain, depression, and anger for those with chronic back pain, according to an organization called A Campaign for Forgiveness. This nonprofit group promotes the scientific study of the power of forgiveness and its impact on those who've had to deal with everything from child abuse to divorce and even murder in their families.

Everett Worthington, executive director of the organization, maintains that holding on to anger and grudges triggers harmful levels of stress by causing blood pressure and heart rates to climb. That, in turn, makes muscles tense, triggering hormonal responses that negatively affect the immune and cardiovascular systems. Other research has shown that forgiveness relieves stress symptoms and promotes healing psychologically and physically. Psychologist Fred Luskin conducts studies on the power of forgiveness at Stanford University. He believes forgiveness produces measurable results for people who have been psychologically damaged. In one of his studies, seventeen adults traumatized by violence in Northern Ireland were given training in forgiveness that included finding new ways to think about the violence they'd witnessed. As the result of their new abilities to practice forgiveness, the test subjects reported, on average, a 35 percent drop in physical stress symptoms and a 37 percent average decrease in psychological "hurt" feelings.

Forgiving doesn't mean forgetting, and it doesn't mean you have to give approval or acceptance of something bad that was done to you. But you can practice forgiveness in a way that allows you to move forward and build something positive as the result of a negative experience. Think about the positive things that can happen by forgiving a spouse who has done you wrong, or a child who has made a mistake, or a coworker who caused more work for you. What's strange is that it is so easy to see the good in forgiveness, but it is so hard for us to practice it. A Gallup Poll study found that 94 percent of Americans surveyed said it was important to forgive, but only 48 percent said they usually tried to do it.

Some people think of forgiveness as a sign of weakness, but it takes strength to control anger and hurt. It takes strength to forgive and move forward. And the results can change the world. One of the best examples of the power of forgiveness is black South Africa's spiritual leader Archbishop Desmond Tutu, who received the 1984 Nobel Peace Prize. Tutu led

South Africa's Truth and Reconciliation Commission, which helped heal the nation after the fall of apartheid. Tutu has noted that forgiveness and reconciliation are not cheap, they are costly. "After all, they cost God the death of God's son," he once said. What I like about Tutu's take on forgiveness and loving your enemies is that he acknowledges that to forgive is not to condone or to minimize the awfulness of an atrocity or wrong that has been done to you. Instead, he says that it is to choose to acknowledge the essential humanity of the perpetrator and to give that perpetrator the possibility of making a new beginning.

Tutu describes forgiveness of an enemy as "an act of much hope and not despair." He teaches that we should have faith in every person's potential to change. Tutu believed that forgiveness was the key to restoring the social equilibrium of South Africa. He has said that the process of reconciliation began when the victims decided to forgive rather than to seek vengeance.

Of course, the man who put the power of forgiveness into practice and changed the world as a result was Tutu's friend Nelson Mandela. He applied the power of forgiveness on a global scale. Mandela and Tutu brought down the evil of apartheid in South Africa by unleashing the full power of their Christian faith and refusing to back down from their belief that all men and women are equal and worthy of God's love and forgiveness.

Mandela's rise from the prison cell to the presidency of his nation may be one of history's greatest examples of the power of God's forgiveness, unconditional love, and the successful application of Christian principles. Though he is often cast in saintly terms, Mandela was in fact a warrior. Those who shared

his views considered him a freedom fighter. Those who op-
posed him considered him a terrorist. Today, however, most
agree that during his imprisonment, Mandela was transformed
so that he rose to an entirely different realm of existence. He
became a man capable of healing nations through the power of
his Christian faith and his belief in Christian principles, particularly God's unconditional love of mankind and womankind.

Mandela stunned friends and foes alike when he emerged
from prison and immediately renounced any thoughts of seeking retribution against those who had imprisoned him. Instead,
he preached reconciliation and forgiveness. He did this both as a
political leader and as an individual. He lunched with his jailers
and prosecutors and had tea with the widow of the architect of
apartheid. Mandela had been a formidable African leader when
he went into prison, and he emerged as a global presence.

Mandela could have won a much earlier release from prison,
but he turned it down because of conditions placed upon his
release by the leaders of apartheid. He understands that there
are no conditions when it comes to God's love, and there
should be none placed upon man's right to freedom either.
Those who've met Mandela speak of his aura of serenity and
peace. That's what comes from living a godly life. It is what all
good Christians should aspire to attain. Sonya and I heard
Mandela speak when he came to Los Angeles in 1990, and we
both remember what a striking figure he was. We felt blessed to
be part of that moment in time. Everyone did. When he got up
to address those assembled, there was total silence. He was regarded as a saint by most of the people there. He had a powerful physical presence matched by the spiritual aura that
emanated from him. Sonya and I were both speechless after the

event. He gave a very elegant, moving speech and it was so inspiring to see blacks and whites rise together to applaud for
this man, who in so many ways showed us the positive benefits
of forgiveness.

The practice of forgiveness is one of the most basic of all
Christian principles, yet I'd neglected it. Jesus tells us through
scripture that we have to forgive others if we want to be forgiven ourselves. "For if you forgive men when they sin against
you, your heavenly Father will also forgive you. But if you do
not forgive men their sins, your Father will not forgive your
sins" (Matthew 6:14–15).

I'd say that's pretty clear, wouldn't you? Still, if we're honest,
most of us have to acknowledge it is darned difficult to put
into application in our down-and-dirty, nitty-gritty daily lives.
God set down some tough rules and then he went and created a
world populated by imperfect people. It is generally not our
nature to immediately forgive someone who has hurt us, disappointed us, used and abused us, humiliated us, taken advantage
of us, stolen from us, or otherwise stepped on our toes. But I
am here to tell you—as one totally fallible and fault-ridden
human being to another—it's achievable through the love and
mercy of God.

With the analyst's guidance, and through many hours of
prayer, I returned to forgiveness as a way of life, and it saved
me. But this story has another twist. There are many forms of
forgiveness beyond that directed at those who've mistreated
you. I had to learn to forgive others, but more important, I
came to forgive myself.

Certainly I was angry at those record company honchos
who apparently thought I was too naïve to run their black

music division. But that was just on the surface. Deeper down, I was even angrier with myself for being all the things they accused me of being—too honest, too moral, too much of a goody-goody to be a player in the high-stakes, recording industry. I wasn't simply angry at them because they were wrong about me. I was angry at myself because I'd let myself believe they were right about me!

God help me! God help all of us! We are imperfect and complicated organisms, we humans. We have layers upon layers upon layers of complex emotions including conflicting fears, insecurities, and all sorts of other crap. My analyst helped me see that in repressing my anger and shoving it into a mental storage closet, I'd lit a slow-burning fuse to self-destruction. I'd closed a door that would have opened to insights of self-awareness. If I'd dealt with my anger at the time, I might have seen, even without professional help, that most of it was directed inward.

The devil was at work, for sure, because he'd pushed my buttons and the self-loathing had kicked in. And you cannot love Jesus if you hate yourself, because we are God's children, created in his image! Satan is sneaky. He was trying to turn me away from God by making me hate myself. He wanted me to self-destruct so that God would have lost another Christian soldier. But like Job, I hung in there with Jesus Christ, the Holy Spirit, and God the Father as my dynamic trio. I did not give up on God even as I was nearly giving up on myself.

Jesus says, "Do unto others as you would have them do unto you." He also says, "Whatever you do to the least of my brothers, you do to me." If we want God to forgive us, we must forgive ourselves. If God loves me, how could I hate myself? If

God is willing to forgive us our sins, then who are we to continue holding on to our own self-condemnation? God pardons our sins when we confess and repent. He knows we are not perfect so he has given us forgiveness as a gift. "I, even I, am he who blots out your transgressions, for my own sake, and remembers your sins no more" (Isaiah 43:25).

As we grow in our faith and become better servants of God, we develop deeper understanding and, hopefully, we also learn to apply his teachings in our daily lives. The Bible tells us that when we are weak, Jesus is strong. The way of Jesus is love, faithfulness, compassion, and forgiveness. Because of this episode with anxiety, I had to change my life and the amount of stress in my life. I learned to pray more frequently and fervently, while asking Jesus to take away my burdens as well as my anger. I finally made up my mind to let go of anger and to go with God instead. It really is a waste of time to pass judgment on yourself or on others, because God is the final judge. He will deal with it, so we should let it go. He is the judge of all people and all things. Scripture says in Isaiah 33:22, "For the LORD is our judge, the LORD is our lawgiver, the LORD is our king; it is he who will save us."

As I've worked on this aspect of my life and my faith, I've found scriptures to help me, such as "Better is the poor that walketh in his uprightness, than he that is perverse in his ways, though he be rich" (Proverbs 28:6, King James Version of the Bible). The NIV Translation is slightly different, but I want to share it with you as well: "Better a poor man whose walk is blameless than a rich man whose ways are perverse."

In hindsight, I realize that the recording industry job I desired so badly truly was not for me. I would have been selling my soul to the devil. I believed that corruption existed in the industry. It always does when there is a lot of money involved. I had wonderful intentions. God had other plans for me. Now I get it. I can only hope and pray that I fulfill God's wishes for me. I want to be the poster child for the good that God is able to do through us when we seek him first in our lives. All any of us can do is hope to change the world by being the best Christians we can be.

I did not become a record company executive. I did not stop rappers from releasing records that exalt decadence and immorality. It would have been one heck of a fight between me and Satan up in that office tower. Instead of fighting those lonely battles, I am blessed to still be broadcasting God's grand gospel music around the world while working, in subtle ways, to serve him with my other syndicated radio shows, too.

Bishop G. E. Patterson sings a great traditional gospel song called "Look Where He Brought Me From." I love this song for its rhythm, the lyrics, and the beauty of the voices in the choir. God's spirit is all over this song. Bishop Patterson is the presiding prelate of the Church of God in Christ. He is pastor of the Temple of Deliverance in Memphis, Tennessee. And when you hear the music performed by him and his congregation, you feel delivered, that's for certain. "Look Where He Brought Me From" is a song of gratitude. When I hear it, I'm grateful for being delivered from the darkness of anger and hurt to the light of forgiveness, thanks to the blessings of his Son, Jesus Christ. God has brought me from the outhouse to the penthouse as one of his chosen servants.

My syndicated radio shows are a great conduit for reaching millions of people with God's music, and his teachings. I'm blessed to have a wonderful partner in Spencer Brown, chairman of Excelsior Radio Networks, who has supported our efforts. An even greater blessing are the faxes, emails, and calls to our Faith Line that reach me from listeners throughout the United States, Canada, the Caribbean, and other countries around the world. God continues to bless me with their support.

God is also working through me now as an ordained minister. I'm on staff at First African Methodist Episcopal Church (FAME), Los Angeles, as one of the associate ministers. Apparently, once I learned to forgive myself, God felt I was ready to serve as one of his representatives on earth.

Praise the LORD. Praise God in his sanctuary; praise him in his mighty heavens. Praise him for his acts of power; praise him for his surpassing greatness. Praise him with the sounding of the trumpet, praise him with the harp and lyre, praise him with tambourine and dancing, praise him with the strings and flute, praise him with the clash of cymbals, praise him with resounding cymbals. Let everything that has breath praise the LORD. Praise the LORD (Psalm 150:1–6).

You're probably wondering, "What ever happened to his poor messed-up finger?" Let me wrap up that loose end for you, because it also contains a message about God's healing ways. Despite all of my mental torment, I did make it to my surgery appointment at the UCLA Medical Center. As I was being prepared to go under the knife, my seasoned surgeon, Dr. Roy Meals, showed up with his entire surgical team. He told me that he'd learned I was a Christian so he asked me to join him and his staff in prayer. As they prayed with me, Dr. Meals put a hand on me. This doctor had more than medical training working for him. He was definitely one of those "healing souls" born to be a physician. I immediately relaxed and felt assured—and this was before the drugs kicked in. I had the sense that the surgeon and his staff had tapped into the healing power of the Holy Spirit. I felt God's presence in the room and I felt a surge of confidence. After that, I had no doubt that the second surgery would restore my finger's range of motion— and it did. I was inspired by this Christian surgeon, a man of God who freely expressed his spiritual beliefs while using his healing gifts and talents.

Dr. Meals's abilities reminded me of Jeremiah 8:22: "Is there no balm in Gilead? Is there no physician there? Why then is there no healing for the wound of my people?"

A caring Christian physician healed my hand and my damaged finger with his medical skills. And a caring God treated my wounded spirit by showing me the power of forgiveness as a healing balm. A famous Negro spiritual, "The Balm of Gilead," is based upon that passage from Jeremiah. Not surprisingly, it is a song of healing and hope, and when I study its lyrics, it too appears to offer us a lesson in the power of forgiveness. It begins:

᧤

There is a balm in Gilead to make
the wounded whole.

᧤

NINE

Fear for the Faithful

GOSPEL OF LOVE:
We should have a respectful fear and awe of God

The fear of the LORD is the beginning of wisdom;
all who follow his precepts have good understanding. To him belongs eternal praise.

—PSALM 111:10

Moses preached: "Fear the Lord all the days of your lives."
Jesus said: "Do not fear, for I am with you."

My Army Airborne Master Sergeant Russell T. Barnes
screamed: "Jump now or I'll throw your butt out!"

We get all sorts of helpful direction on the subject of fear,
don't we? As Christians practicing our faith in a sometimes
hostile or uncaring secularized world, how do we handle fear?
In our faith do we live in fear of God? Or do we reject fear because God is our benevolent heavenly father who protects us?
Or both? And in our daily lives do we embrace fear because it
keeps us on the straight and narrow? Or do we try to live fear-
lessly? We certainly can't avoid it because fear is sewn into the

fabric of life just as it is part of the cloth of our faith. In our Bible readings we find fear on page after page. Reading along, we discover Abraham lying out of fear, Jacob fearing Esau, Moses fearing the pharaoh, and the disciples fearing storms, soldiers, and even Jesus, whom they mistake for a ghost. This semicomic moment occurs in Matthew 14:26 when the poor disciples spot Jesus walking on the lake's surface: "'It's a ghost,' they said and cried out in fear."

Even without being witness to a miracle, it is not unusual for Christians to feel overwhelmed and fearful at the thought of God's presence and his power. And when we stumble in our efforts to lead Christian lives, we may want to run from our faith because we don't want God to punish us. We know he can cut us off. God can stop us in our tracks. He can take us out! So we can have these conflicting feelings of both attraction to God and dread of his power. This is what the theologian Rudolf Otto referred to as the *mysterium tremendum et fascinans*, which is Latin for the "fearful and fascinating mystery." It is the awe-filled experience of the majesty of God. It can be overpowering and yet enrapturing, both thrilling and chilling, according to Otto. But we can't walk away from our faith in him. Not for long. Because life always brings us back around. There is no going it alone.

We Need God

Oddly enough, fear plays a role also in one of the most comforting and joyous scenes in the Bible. It occurs in John 20:19 on the evening of the day of resurrection when the disciples are gathered together shocked at the news that Jesus' tomb is empty. They are frightened that their Jewish opponents may come after them so they have locked the doors, but suddenly Jesus appears in their midst and greets them. John tells us that "On the evening of that first day of the week, when the disciples were together with the doors locked for fear of the Jews, Jesus came and stood among them and said, 'Peace be with you!'" It's no coincidence that we use that same greeting today in many Christian services. We all want to be comforted from our daily fears and worries. We all want to practice and worship our God in peace.

Fear Factors

Yet we face fears of varying intensity throughout our lives, from the fear of mean kids on the playground to the fear of being fired by our bosses or the fear of losing loved ones. Like you, I've dealt with a range of fears. I've learned to manage some, ignore others, and respect those that keep me on path to my Christian goals. You cannot always control the fears that crop up on your walk with God, but you can control how you respond to them. As a Christian, I fear the power of God and his wrath, and that is a fear I welcome because it helps to keep me on course. Yet as a child of a loving God, I know that he will protect me too.

I knew fear as a Pennsylvania country boy who dealt with the usual bullies, racists, and boogeymen under the bed. I spent many dark, eerie nights walking and trying to hitch rides in rural western Pennsylvania after football and basketball games in high school. My adrenaline pumped as I followed the road through the thick woods. I was still keyed up from the games so my senses were on high alert as I walked. In my mind, I played out scenarios of attackers leaping out of the shadows so that I was ready to go ten rounds if anyone did appear. It wasn't unusual to encounter night hunters and other wanderers in those woods. Folks always said, "Anything can happen in these mountains." And it was true. My great-grandmother used to always caution me to be prepared for bad things so that my fears didn't overwhelm me when I needed to defend myself. "Butch, do what you have to do to take care of yourself, son. Don't you let anyone hurt you."

Grandmother Susie was a solid woman of God who believed in taking care of yourself spiritually, physically, financially, socially, and mentally. I live by her words of wisdom to this day. Yet, I didn't have to handle any truly serious fears until early in my military career. I knew fear when I stood on the training platform at paratrooper jump school and looked down. I'd never been that high off the ground in my life. I'd tried to prepare myself by thinking that it couldn't be any worse than leaping off the roof of our one-story house, which I did all the time as a boy—with my guardians yelling that I was going to break a leg one day. I'd gone into the military with a lot of self-confidence. I'd been chosen for the all-state teams in both football and basketball, so I was physically fit and tough mentally. I'd prided myself in running through, not around, my opponents in football, so I wasn't one to avoid challenges. In the backwoods, children were encouraged to face fears because country folks have to depend on their own resourcefulness. Help was often a long way away. In hard times or emergencies, it was often just you and God out there.

Fear of Falling

That was the fearless mind-set I took into the military, but once I put on the uniform, it was a whole new ball game. Paratrooper training gave a lot of brave men and women wobbly knees and second thoughts. That first jump that we were required to take off a thirty-four-foot tower set the tone. The fear factor was off the charts. Either you jumped on your own or you had to turn around and walk back down the stairs and face a gauntlet of derision.

As I recall, we did about five weeks of training in jump school back then. We'd start out jumping off platforms about five feet high to learn techniques for the parachute landing falls. We also did intense physical training to get our bodies in shape by running and doing push-ups, squats, and other exercises designed to build endurance and strength. So the first big test of your courage and willpower was "the Tower." It is thirty-four feet high, which doesn't sound like much until you are standing up there looking down. (You aren't supposed to look down, but of course, you can't help but do it.)

We jumped attached to tension lines that kept us from splattering all over army property, but it still was a scary thing, especially the first time. I had fears, but it helped when I looked down and saw all the guys who had made it before me. It really sunk in then that being a paratrooper was going to require a mastery of many fears. Jump school was not for the faint of heart. If you couldn't find a way to manage your fears, you didn't make it.

My jump school class was about five hundred people at the start and probably only about two hundred made it through. It wasn't just the jumping that weeded them out. There was some serious physical exertion required. We had to run everywhere, from long cross-country runs to sprints to the mess hall and the latrine. You ran everywhere. If you didn't run, your drill sergeants made you do push-ups or some other form of fitness torture. The first jump off the thirty-four-foot platform was a rite of passage conducted as a solemn ritual. We were supposed to maintain quiet as we walked up the stairway, but there was a lot of whispering, muttering, nervous joking, teasing, and praying going on to overcome fears. There were jumpmasters at the top and bottom offering their own choice words of encouragement, or disparagement, depending on which way you were going—up or down the stairs. They screamed at us at the top because we were supposed to be getting accustomed to thinking clearly in stressful situations. They didn't yell at you by name. You were a number instead. You weren't called by your name until you made it through jump school. I was 17, the number taped to my helmet.

"Seventeen, are you ready to jump or are you gonna cry for your momma? Are you gonna jump or are you gonna punk out?"

I was eager to prove that I could do it, so between prayers I answered, "No, sergeant, I'm going to jump, sergeant!"

The jumpmaster then hooked me up to the suspension lines, ran through my equipment check with me, told me to stand in the door, look out at the horizon (not down!), and when he said go, I went. Following my training, I leapt out as far as I could go into the wide open space. Then I waited and waited for the suspension lines to catch. I counted one thousand one, one thousand two, one thousand three and finally, my body was jolted as the suspension lines simulated the feeling of

a parachute opening and slowing the descent. You actually slide down the long suspension line and gradually you slow down so that the people at the bottom can stop you as you reach the ground, so it is not quite the same feel of a real parachute drop. But it was close enough for me.

It was a scary thing and I had to fight my natural fear of heights as well as my natural fear of hitting the ground at a high rate of speed. But once I made it, I was elated. The Twenty-third Psalm tended to run through this Christian soldier's mind quite frequently during my paratrooper training and throughout my nearly seven-year military career. Knowing that God was with me helped a great deal, but as I found myself jumping, rather than walking, into the valley of the shadow of death, I also hoped that he had a backup parachute handy, along with his rod and staff. Yes, I had some serious fear facing to do before I made the leap of faith with only those tension lines and my faith in God offering hope of salvation.

First, there was the fear of jumping off that platform. Then there was the fear of what would happen to me if I didn't jump. Being branded a coward in the military is totally unacceptable, and in the airborne it is not tolerated. I had heard about what happens if a trainee decided to quit jump school. It seemed very clear that you were better off just throwing yourself off a cliff. Later, I saw guys get up there and refuse to go through with it. They would have to go back down the stairs with hundreds of soldiers jeering them. Their drill sergeants were at the bottom of the stairs. The "washouts" would have to declare that they would not jump off the tower. They would then be forced to crawl across the sand and rocks to the com-

manding officer's headquarters while more soldiers and drill sergeants screamed at them. It was hellish, and it was intended to inspire fear in all of us. We did not want to fail as soldiers in the military because of those fears—just as our fear of God makes us want to stay on the righteous path.

When we learn to manage or conquer or live with fears and to channel them into positive energy, the rewards are plentiful, both on earth and in heaven. My reward for conquering my fears as a paratrooper came on jump school graduation day. Our training required us to do five jumps to qualify for our wings. The final jump is part of the graduation day celebration with our families and loved ones invited to watch from the grandstands. My mother was there for the occasion. She was worried that she would not be able to pick me out when the skies filled with hundreds of parachutes, so she gave me a beautiful, bright blue scarf to wave at her. One of my drill sergeants saw me with it just before I got on the plane. I thought he was going to tear into me and make me throw it in the trash, but instead, he told me to hide it until I got on the plane and then to have a buddy tie it around my arm for me. I followed his instructions, and when I came floating down to earth, I waved my arm and my mother saw me and announced to everyone, "There's my son!"

Bible Bravery

I made it through my military years only because God watched over me and gave me the intestinal fortitude to do it. I was way out of my country boy comfort zone. With God as a daily presence in your life, you can do anything.

"I can do everything through him who gives me strength" (Philippians 4:13).

You simply have to trust in him. Christians have an advantage in these situations because we learn so much about fear from the Bible. It is not a foreign concept to us. We have many great examples of courage to follow, most notably that of the Son of God who suffered for our sins. In the Bible, we are taught that the only fear we should have is the fear of the Lord. With a lot of help from the Bible and my Christian training, I learned to "manage" my fear in the military from my first day of boot camp when it got right up in my face and stayed there. There were drill sergeants screaming, yelling, and spitting froth on us constantly. But most of us understood there was a motive for this madness. They want you to learn how to think, react, and perform properly in high-stress situations because that is what you would have to do in combat. You are trained to manage your fears and to channel the fight-or-flight energy generated into strength, speed, and mental alertness.

One of my drill sergeants offered us a little paternal advice in telling us that there is no shame in being afraid of something, but that we have to learn to conquer our fears so that we can function and protect each other in combat situations. His advice reminded me of Psalm 111:10: "The fear of the Lord is the beginning of wisdom." Once you understand the source of your fears and embrace them, you gain wisdom that helps you function at a higher level in every aspect of your life. It is good to fear the Lord as long as you are not paralyzed by that fear, just as it is good for a child to fear his parents at a certain level, but not in such a way that love and affection and understanding are lost.

THE GOSPEL ACCORDING TO REV. WALT "BABY" LOVE

Later, I was grateful for my fear management training many times in the jungles of northeastern Thailand, a place where, officially, there were no U.S. soldiers at that time. Air bases, yes. But not us! We were a little-known operation called "The 9th Log" (short for Logistical Command). We were part of the Military Advisory Command Vietnam. During most of my thirteen-month tour, I felt relatively secure within the camp, but we were surrounded by Vietnamese, Cambodian, and Laotian guerrillas so there was always a threat of a surprise attack springing out of the jungle. It was a long way from the hills and forests of my boyhood, so much so that we referred to the United States as "the world" and our surroundings as something beyond it.

Fear of Flunking

The fear of being out of your comfort zone, in an unfamiliar situation or place, can be a healthy fear because it keeps you alert and cautious. It is harmful, however, if it debilitates or paralyzes you. This type of fear, a fear of failing, is related to survival. It can freeze up some people because they equate failure with death. Only in certain situations does failure mean death, but those who overreact to their fears of failure tend to see that as the possible outcome in every stressful situation. We are warned against that sort of paralyzed reaction to fear in Proverbs 3:25–26: "Have no fear of sudden disaster or of the ruin that overtakes the wicked, for the Lord will be your confidence and will keep your foot from being snared."

In recent years, I grappled with a type of fear that was very different from anything I experienced in the military. I had to deal with the fear of failing when I entered the seminary at the age of fifty-seven. For all of the challenges I'd faced as an athlete, as a soldier, and as a broadcaster, I'd never been as intimidated as when I stepped onto the Pasadena campus of the Fuller Theological Seminary. Founded in 1947, it is regarded as one of the top seminaries in the world, and it appealed to me on a couple levels. I'd always wanted to get a college degree by studying theology at a great school. Fuller immediately felt like home, especially after I learned that one of the cofounders was Charles E. Fuller, a famous radio evangelist. I felt God had chosen Fuller Theological Seminary for me also when I learned of a Fuller program that almost seemed designed specifically for me.

In 1973, Fuller had begun a theological studies program for minority ministers. It offered master's level degrees even to those who aspired to the ministry but had not had the opportunity to complete a standard baccalaureate degree. Hundreds of African Americans have benefited from the African American Church Studies program at Fuller. Still, it is one thing to go to college when you are young and full of energy and unencumbered by other responsibilities; it's another thing to go in as a husband, father, primary figure in your own internationally syndicated radio show production company, and as an editor of a very powerful music and radio industry trade publication.

It was exciting and invigorating in many ways to go back to school at that age—and it was scary as scary can be in many others. It was also very humbling. There I was, a fairly accomplished man who'd built a very successful multimedia career with a business of my own. I certainly didn't need the extra work. But suddenly, I was a "freshman again." Actually I was a graduate student, but I felt like a freshman, and one of the most senior freshmen at that. Theological schools tend to draw an older group of students in general, but the majority of the students were a good twenty years younger than me. I was older than more than a few of my instructors too. It made for some interesting dynamics. In addition, for reasons that drove my wife to distraction, I decided to also go through ministerial training for the African Methodist Episcopal Church while attending night classes at Fuller—and I kept my day job too. For four and a half years, I worked all day in broadcasting, recording four radio shows and dealing with my usual workload, and then I attended graduate-school-level seminary classes from 6:00 P.M. until 10:00 P.M. at night. After that, I went home and did my homework, writing papers, reading books for two different schools and two different course loads into the wee hours of the morning.

Lessons in Humility

Sonya tried to discourage me from taking all this on at once. But I had another fear that I was dealing with. I knew God had called me to the ministry and I was afraid that if I didn't get my degree quickly I might die or run out of energy before I could answer his call. There were plenty of nights when I prayed to God saying, "Lord, you got me into this, so please grant me the strength to get through it." There were times also when I became very discouraged. It was the "old dog, new tricks" thing. My first class at Fuller was in the New Testament. Matthew, Mark, Luke, and John were old friends. I'd been reading them for years. But I'd never "studied" their gospels so intensely from a scholarly perspective. I had a professor who must have been a drill sergeant earlier in life. I fully expected him to order me to drop and give him fifty paragraphs at any second. He'd have me write on very challenging topics and then he'd dock me points for having a semicolon where he felt a comma would do. I'd only been writing a column for a national trade publication for about twenty years at that point, so there was not a lot of rust on my keyboard. I knew what I was doing. But academics are a strange breed. They write in their own language, which is generally unintelligible to people who approach reading and writing as mere communication. I wrote in a conversational manner, which was far too uncomplicated for my professor. At one point, I even asked him to meet me for lunch, hoping I could win him over. He admitted during our talk that my research was well done, my reports were accurate, and that I clearly understood the material.

"You just have to learn to write," he said.

That was one of those days when I felt that I'd walked through a portal into an alternate universe. Writing wasn't writing as I knew it in his world. So I had to learn to write *his* way in order to keep my grades up to stay in the graduate school program at Fuller. It was humbling, but maybe that was part of God's plan for me too. I was being challenged and knocked out of my comfort zone, perhaps so I would encounter and learn to face new fears so that I might better serve him as a minister.

It helped that in my studies, I often came across biblical passages that bolstered me and helped me deal with the challenges of my schoolwork. I found many on fear, including some that reminded me of the fact that while other people can make things difficult for us here in the world, they are no threat in the hereafter. Jesus was referring to that when he said: "Do not be afraid of those who kill the body but cannot kill the soul. Rather, be afraid of the One who can destroy both soul and body in hell" (Matthew 10:28).

One of my favorite scriptures strengthened me when fears of failing arose. It is found in 2 Timothy 1:7. The Apostle Paul was a father figure for Timothy, who had been raised by his grandmother Lois and his mother Eunice. Both were strong Christians and friends of Paul. Timothy was preaching the gospel but ran into difficulties because some felt he was too young to be teaching, preaching, and leading others in the ways of Christ Jesus. Paul was trying to encourage Timothy to stay strong in the spirit even under the mounting pressures of people opposing him and persecuting him. The King James Version reports that Paul said: "For God hath not given us the spirit of fear; but of power, and of love, and of a sound mind." The NIV Translation has this interpretation: "For God did not give us a spirit of timidity, but a spirit of power, of love and of self-discipline." I also like the Amplified Bible's translation of the original Greek in this case: "For God did not give us a spirit of timidity (of cowardice, of craven and cringing and fawning fear), but [He has given us a spirit] of power and of love and of calm and well-balanced mind and discipline and self-control."

Paul was telling Timothy—and us—to be strong and steadfast in our faith in God through Jesus Christ. We've got to be more in awe of God than of man and his threats toward us when it comes to our standing up for who and what we are as

Christians. Hebrews 13:6 reminds us: "So we say with confidence, the LORD is my helper; I will not be afraid. What can man do to me?"

Finishing Well

I became very adept at praying while I studied, and studying while I prayed. I got through my seminary studies by channeling the energy of my fear of failing into determination. Once I started grad school at Fuller, I was not going to embarrass myself. Nor was I going to disappoint Prophet Johnson or any of the others who had encouraged me to pursue the ministry. I truly felt called to it by God. He doesn't play around; I wasn't playing either. But I was praying. Oh yes, I prayed for God's help all the way through those four and a half years, and I needed his blessings every minute of the way.

It was a challenge all the way through to the last day of the last class. In fact, my final class may well have been the toughest, as well as the most interesting. It was a renowned course called Lifelong Development taught by J. Robert "Bobby" Clinton, professor of leadership at Fuller, who has written many books drawn upon his scholarship and his experiences as a missionary. This fascinating course looks at how Christian leaders are developed by studying the life histories of more than nine hundred biblical, historical, and contemporary leaders. In the class, we defined a Christian leader as someone with a God-given capacity and God-given responsibility who influences God's people for God's purposes. We also learned that God tests his Christian leaders for strength of character and integrity. Those who respond well continue to grow as leaders, while those who do not rise to the challenge will be tested until they do. I felt I was being tested as a future leader even as I studied the process. Professor Clinton teaches that the development of a leader takes a lifetime and that God shapes the character, skills, and values of his leaders on earth. We learned to see patterns in the way God develops leaders, and to recognize the values and lessons of God's process for developing leadership skills. One of the great things about this course was that we had to analyze our own lives using the tools and concepts taught by Professor Clinton. I learned a great deal not only about many Christian leaders but also about myself and what I need to correct from my past in order to move forward. Professor Clinton struck a chord when he said that we need to listen to what God wants to do through us and then trust him to do it. After all, that's why I was at Fuller taking his class. He also taught that it is important for Christians to "finish well" in their lives, and he provided examples of both those who did and those who did not. It was fitting, then, that this was the last class I had to pass to get my graduate degree. I certainly wanted to finish well, but I had one heck of a time doing it.

One of my primary challenges was more of a technical problem than an intellectual one. Professor Clinton was a convert in a certain regard, and like most converts, he wanted to share his newfound enthusiasm. He was a convert to computers and their technology. He told us that he had avoided using personal computers until three years earlier, but once he discovered their usefulness, he became avid about them. He wanted all of his students to learn to use the technology that he had embraced. I'd been something of a holdout too. I had been doing basic word processing stuff on personal computers for a while, but I'd generally disdained email and a lot of the other technology because it only seemed to add to my workload. I tried email for a while, but I'd get more than eighty emails a day from listeners and business associates and scam artists and spammers. It just ate up my time, so I quit messing with it.

But Professor Clinton wanted us to email our daily assignments to him and he wanted us to download material from a disk onto our computers, so I had to go with his program. I had a laptop and started using it for class, but I had some real problems with it, particularly when it came to downloading material from the disks that Professor Clinton had us purchase. For some reason, my laptop seemed to balk at reading those disks—usually at very critical times when I had to get something done on deadline.

If God tests his chosen leaders, then I must have been one of the chosen because I was sorely tested in that class. I can laugh about it now—barely—but back then when I was feeling the pressure of getting through one final class and dealing with my fear of computer technology, I freaked out on a regular basis. I had some major panic attacks while wrestling with my laptop, which provided my computer-savvy wife and son no end of amusement. I was blessed, though, because I remembered to apply the things I was learning from Professor Clinton as I was learning them. He believes that Christian leaders have to regularly ask God's help and guidance if they are to succeed. And, Lord knows, I did a lot of praying for help and guidance. At one point, I had a ten-page paper to write for class the next day and I became so frustrated with my balky laptop that I ran out of the house, stood in the driveway, raised my arms and eyes to heaven, and said, "Oh God, I'm so close to completing my seminary work, please show me how to get this computer to read the disk so I can graduate and serve you at a higher level!"

God answered my prayers by hooking me up with some younger guys in the class, real solid Christians who were more computer savvy. They were very patient and helpful in showing me how to download off the informational disk from the professor. Eventually, I overcame my fears of computer technology and survived this test from God and moved forward in my lifelong journey to be a Christian leader by earning my degree from Fuller.

When I was anxious about my last assignment in seminary, I prayed and asked God to help me. Only then did anxiety leave me. I returned to a sound mind and a peaceful spirit, which helped me complete my work for the course. The Lifelong Development class that brought on all this anxiety was an *intensive class.* It was an accelerated course of study that offered a ten-week class taught in ten days! I was saying some hallelujahs to make it through that challenging course. I was just hoping to do well enough to pass and get the four units needed for graduation. My class adviser had recommended that I take it as a pass/fail class to take off some of the pressure because I was getting burned out with my class workload on top of my real world workload. I was going to class mostly two or three nights a week; doing four radio shows per week; conducting three services at First A.M.E. (FAME) Church each Sunday; taking communion to the elderly and sick at their homes each month; and also struggling to hold up my end as a husband and father. So I went with the pass/fail system on that class. Even though it had me worried, I got it together. As it says in Romans 8:28. "All things work together for good." I graded out with an A–, which did not count toward my GPA. But, praise the Lord, I passed the course. If only I'd had less fear and more faith. The faith of a mustard seed? Maybe, just maybe. In the Bible, we are told that the only fear we should have is the fear of the Lord. He is God Almighty: the Triune Godhead, God the Father, God the Son, and God the Holy Spirit. The lesson I've drawn from my readings and study is that we should have a respectful fear of God in much the way that a child respects a parent. We have the free will choice of believing that Jesus Christ is Lord, the Son of God. He is the truth and the life and the door to the Father. Scripture tells us in Jesus' own words recorded in John 14:6: Jesus answered, "I am the way and the truth and the life. No one comes to the Father except through me."

I don't know how I made it through that final class at Fuller. I thank God for giving me the perseverance. The Bible tells us in Romans 5:3–5 that we should rejoice in our sufferings because suffering produces perseverance that produces character that produces hope. There were many nights when I drove home after class praying for perseverance and thanking God for helping me keep on keeping on. On those trips, I often listened to the gospel music of Keith "Wonderboy" Johnson & the Spiritual Voices. Their song "I Thank You For What You've Done" gave me the attitude of gratitude that I needed to do just that. Gospel music is truly a blessing because it helps keep the flames of Christian faith burning in us.

I love reading the book of Proverbs. Even though I've read it a number of times, there's always something that jumps off the page at you, some uncovered nugget to learn from. Proverbs 9:10 is another enlightening offering: "The fear of the LORD is the beginning of wisdom, and knowledge of the Holy One is understanding." And Proverbs 10:27 offers that: "The fear of the LORD adds length to life, but the years of the wicked are cut short." Passage after passage in the Bible encourages us to have a healthy fear and awe of God. Yet we are also comforted in the knowledge that if we walk the Christian path, he will protect us.

Jesus was obedient to his Father and was willing to die on the cross for our sins. He became our redeeming and atoning sacrifice to God. He is our salvation if we repent of our sins, confess with our mouths that Jesus Christ is our Lord and Savior, and are baptized. We will have life everlasting. Jesus said: "Do not fear, for I am with you." I encourage you to do as I do when other fears arise. Look to the Bible and pray for God's protection. I take particular comfort in reading John 14:27 when Jesus said, "Peace I leave with you; my peace I give you. I do not give to you as the world gives. Do not let your hearts be troubled and do not be afraid."

The next time your fears catch up with you, remember these words from Isaiah 33:6: "He will be the sure foundation for your times, a rich store of salvation and wisdom and knowledge; the fear of the Lord is the key to this treasure."

✌

"Do not be anxious about anything, but in everything, by prayer and petition, with thanksgiving, present your request to God. And the peace of God, which transcends all understanding, will guard your hearts and your minds in Christ Jesus."
—PHILIPPIANS 4:6–7

✌

TEN

Sharing God's Blessings

GOSPEL OF LOVE:

Charity and love are essential to our faith

"When you reap the harvest of your land, do not
reap to the very edges of your field or gather the
gleanings of your harvest. Leave them for the poor
and the alien. I am the LORD your God."

—LEVITICUS 23:22

I felt confusion and resentment as a child standing in line at the
AFL-CIO Union Hall in New Kensington, Pennsylvania. My
great-grandmother Susie and my granddad Davis got me up too
early for my taste. It didn't make sense that we had to hurry to
catch a bus from Creighton, so we could wait in a long line. My
great-grandparents told me to be patient. We were waiting to get
"surplus food." I could not understand why we needed to stand
in line for food. We had food at home. There were groceries and
markets nearby. My grandfather had a steady job in the glass
factory. Why would my great-grandparents make such an effort
to get so little just because it was being given away?

At the time, I had no concept of what it was to be "working poor," but that was our economic status. My great-grandfather did have a steady job, but his wages were so low that we still qualified for government food programs. As a boy brought up to be self-reliant, I came to resent the fact that we were considered "needy." That resentment undoubtedly helped to fuel my determined drive as an athlete who had to be the best, and later as an adult striving for career success and financial security. Yet before I learned to channel my resentment in a constructive way, I felt stigmatized and ashamed that others viewed us as reliant on handouts and the charity of others. Other kids would go by—kids that I knew from school or sports—and they'd yell things, point, and laugh.

"Hey, poor boy, you waitin' for some cheese?"

I could only take it so long before I'd yell things back at them and threaten to do them bodily harm. That only succeeded in embarrassing my great-grandparents.

"Hush, boy! Don't let ignorant people get under your skin. Be a gentleman. You know better. Christians don't act like that," my great-grandmother would say.

It was humiliating, and obviously it is an experience I have never forgotten. My feelings of resentment and embarrassment were understandable given my age and my lack of awareness, but they were also simply wrong. You see, my great-grandparents really didn't haul off to the union hall to get surplus food and other goods for us. We were mostly there to pick up supplies that my great-grandmother passed out to even needier families and individuals who could not make the trip or could not collect enough to feed all of their own family members. We were there mostly on a charitable mission. It was in-

credible how much food we'd get each month from the surplus program. We'd come home with bag after bag packed with flour, powdered milk, margarine, butter, Spam, potted meat, pork and beans, dried beans, and boxes of cheese. I will confess that as much as I hated the image of being poor and standing in that surplus food line, I dearly loved the grilled surplus cheese sandwiches that my great-grandmother made for me. My mouth still waters at the memory of those sweet-smelling sandwiches.

My guardians, God bless them, gave away most of what we'd haul home on the bus. There'd come a knock on the door and my great-grandmother would grab handfuls of goods to pass out. Or she'd call to me for help, load boxes and bags into my arms, and lead me through the neighborhood to our delivery destination. The remarkable thing was that I also saw my great-grandparents slip cash, along with the food, to those they were helping. I also overheard their conversations in which they deliberated over how much they could afford to give from their last ten or twenty dollars before the next payday at the glass plant.

My great-grandparents lived their Christian faith through their deeds. And giving to others was perhaps their most powerful expression of their Christianity. In James 2:20–26, the apostle explains that faith and actions work together. By living our faith with Christian actions, we are complete. James notes that "faith alone" is not enough. "As the body without the spirit is dead, so faith without deeds is dead," he writes.

My great-grandparents were practicing their Christian faith through deeds done with love at the deepest, most heartfelt level. It was the poor helping the poor, the needy helping those with just a little more need. If bread was all we had, we shared bread. If we had only crumbs, then crumbs we shared. Sometimes it was just the warmth of a stove or the comfort of a bed, or a little company on a bad night; whatever little they had to give, my great-grandparents gave in abundance. And I learned more about being a true Christian from them than I ever could have from all of my studies of the Bible or in seminary school. My great-grandparents lived according to God's teachings. Their unselfish and pure displays of charity were among their greatest gifts to me. They always told me that it was a blessing for them to be able to help others. It was just another way for them to express gratitude to God for his grace and mercy in their lives, they said.

In early Bible translations, the Greek word *agape* was translated as *caritas* and defined as an expression of love in the fullest. Later, *caritas* evolved to mean "the giving of goods to feed the poor" or "tolerance in judging others" and lost some of its connotation of deep Christian love. As a result, newer English translations of the Bible substitute *love* for *charity (caritas)* in many passages. That is why if you go looking for the familiar phrase "faith, hope, and charity," in many newer translations of I Corinthians 13:13, you will find instead, "faith, hope, and love."

I understand the reasoning behind the change in translation, but in some ways, it is a shame because I believe true Christian charity is an expression of love in its fullest sense—love of God and man. We learn in the Bible that a great mind and a wealth of knowledge are of no value without a benevolent and charitable—loving—heart. "Doing good" is not good enough if it is not done out of love for God and his people. When I think of true charity as an expression of love, I'm always reminded of the unselfishness of my great-grandparents, and particularly my great-grandmother Susie. She was a matriarch with God-given wisdom, power, faith, love, perseverance, and strength. She held our family together in a Christlike manner all the days of her life. When I think of her and say her name the tears well up in my eyes. I'm compelled to praise the Lord and to shout out his name because his love was manifested in and through her. Hallelujah! Hallelujah! Hallelujah! Glory to his name!

Folks back in Creighton, Pennsylvania, and in surrounding communities for miles around still remember my great-grandmother for her loving acts of charity throughout the Allegheny Kiski Valley area of western Pennsylvania. It's very easy to forget or just choose not to remember our humble beginnings and tougher times in life. I enjoy reflecting on those times because it keeps me grounded in the Lord. If God had not been on my side and put me in the care of my great-grandparents, I'd have been toast. Caput. Done. Over and out! But God was good to me. One of his gifts sent through my great-grandparents was to teach me at an early age about giving to others without expectation. At a time when many wealthy people seek publicity for themselves when they make charitable donations—even to the point of demanding that buildings, streets, or programs be named for them—I can't help but be even more impressed by the quiet and humble charity practiced by my great-grandparents. And I'm sure Jesus would be pleased too, given his remarks in Matthew 6:1–4 when he warns us to "be careful not to do your 'acts of righteousness' before men, to be seen by them. If you do, you will have no reward from your Father in heaven."

No Trumpets

Matthew also cautions that "when you give to the needy, do not announce it with trumpets." Instead, he advises us to give quietly: "do not let your left hand know what your right hand is doing, so that your giving may be in secret. Then your Father, who sees what is done in secret, will reward you."

My parents were not alone in their quiet, charitable ways, of course. Not everyone who lived in our neighborhood was a Christian. We had our share of both sinners and saints. Yet most in the community were willing to step up and share or give whatever they could when they saw a need. They understood hardship because most lived with it, yet they helped each other in a manner that you are not likely to see in most affluent gated communities or subdivisions. This spirit of Christian fellowship is reflected in Acts 2:44–47:

> All the believers were together and had everything in common. Selling their possessions and goods, they gave to anyone as he had need. Every day they continued to meet together in the temple courts. They broke bread in their homes and ate together with glad and sincere hearts, praising God and enjoying the favor of all the people. And the Lord added to their number daily those who were being saved.

I believe God puts us in place to help others. It's not just coincidence that my great-grandparents lived as they did. It was their destiny under God's plan for them. In 2 Corinthians

9:6–8, the Apostle Paul offers a lesson about the importance of helping others.

> *Remember this: Whoever sows sparingly will also reap sparingly, and whoever sows generously will also reap generously. Each man should give what he has decided in his heart to give, not reluctantly or under compulsion, for God loves a cheerful giver. And God is able to make all grace abound to you, so that in all things at all times, having all that you need, you will abound in every good work.*

Sowing Generously

God tells us to take care of the widows and the orphans and the poor. We can all do that in some manner. True Christians can always find a way to share their blessings, even when they have few comforts or pennies to spare. I witnessed acts of charity every day even as I grew up in rural poverty among those often considered to be the poorest of the poor. I saw charity in the form of shared meals, a cup of coffee, a slice of bread, a can of beans, a ride into town, and a hand with a chore. To me, those acts rank above the more recognized and acclaimed charities of billionaires giving millions and millionaires giving hundreds of thousands.

The people of our rural enclave did not give to others to gain recognition for themselves. Many gave out of pure Christian instinct because they saw a need. I can't tell you how many times I heard my great-grandparents or others in our hardscrabble community say they wanted to share God's blessings. Others might look at them and wonder, How are they blessed? They live in shanties. They have no indoor plumbing. They live from paycheck to paycheck. Generation after generation they struggled to put food on the table. But my great-grandparents and many others were truly blessed by the depth of their faith. They always found ways to express their gratitude for God's blessings through charity.

Angels in Our Midst

In a world where people often are portrayed as obsessed with the accumulation of worldly goods, status, and power, the good works and charitable giving of true Christians is often overlooked. Yet there are thousands of God-loving men and women who take time away from their own lives, sacrifice, and quietly give of their talents to help others without earning a dime in return. Armies of these unselfish, heroic Christian soldiers can be found now along the hurricane-ravaged coasts of Louisiana, Mississippi, Alabama, and Florida. They are helping to rebuild homes and restore lives up and down that region in an unprecedented display of Christian charity that is a marvel to behold.

Churches, relief organizations, and Christian groups across the country have dispatched workers to lend a hand since Katrina struck in the fall of 2005, killing at least 1,209 people in Louisiana, Mississippi, Alabama, and Florida. But few people realize that there were already armies of recovery workers from Christian organizations working in Florida to help residents there recover from the hurricanes of 2004. Even before that, they were working at Ground Zero in New York City, helping with the recovery from the September 11, 2001, disaster.

In fact, I'm proud to tell you that in recent years these relief workers have stepped up and succeeded in many areas where government emergency aid programs have fallen short or failed miserably. It is easy to understand why. The Christian volunteers poured into those regions out of love, not duty or ambition.

The work that they have done and that they continue to do never ceases to amaze those who benefit from it. One of my favorite news reports on this Christian phenomenon quoted an eighty-year-old woman in a wheelchair in Pensacola, Florida, who one day found a Michigan dairyman putting new shingles on her storm-damaged roof and a Virginia poultry farmer putting new siding on her home. She had no idea that they were Christian volunteers who'd come with their faith-based relief organization to help victims of Hurricane Ivan.

Still, she told a reporter, "They are angels in our midst."

She was not alone in her moving assessment. Residents and officials along Florida's Panhandle coast were often overwhelmed with emotions upon seeing one truckload of volunteers after another pull into their leveled communities and set to work with no expectations for earthly compensation.

"In the very beginning a recovery expert told us, 'You people can go home. The faith-based community is going to rebuild your town,'" Pensacola, Florida, resident Garrett Walton told a newspaper reporter. "I thought that was the most ridiculous thing I'd ever heard in my life, but I've found out it was true."

I couldn't possibly name all of the faith-based groups working in areas hit by disaster these days, but I do know that among them are wonderful organizations such as Habitat for Humanity, Christian Disaster Response International, Christian Reformed World Relief Committee, Episcopal Relief and

Development, Lutheran Disaster Response, Mennonite Disaster Service, Nazarene Disaster Response, the United Methodist Committee on Relief, the Christian Contractors Association, Churches of Christ Disaster Relief Effort, and International Orthodox Christian Charities. If you ever find yourself wondering if the world has gotten cynical and self-centered beyond salvation, I urge you to simply look at that list and consider the thousands of men and women who take time from their own lives to help relieve the suffering of storm victims. Some rotate in and out, spending a few weeks or months, yet others devote themselves full-time to doing God's work with hammer and nails, working long hours, sleeping in makeshift shelters, and asking for nothing in return.

It is also heartening to see teenagers and young adults have caught the spirit of true Christian charity. Thousands of them have been spending their spring breaks and other free time working in areas hit by disaster. Instead of sunning on the beaches or partying, these young people are cleaning mud and muck out of damaged homes, clearing tons of debris, repairing roofs, and otherwise contributing whatever they can to those who need all the help they can get. Campus Crusade for Christ alone sent nearly eight thousand students to help hurricane victims in the Gulf of Mexico during spring break 2005. Habitat for Humanity hosted another ten thousand students who joined its efforts during their vacations. Lutheran Disaster Response brought in another eleven hundred young volunteers to work in disaster recovery along the coast.

Without a doubt, the expression of love of God in and through us, as his people, can change the world. We must have the faith, the courage, the perseverance, the wisdom, the love of humanity, and the will to express that love as a force for good through charitable actions. Jesus told us we can ask anything in his name and his Father would give it to us as his followers. "In that day you will no longer ask me anything. I tell you the truth, my Father will give you whatever you ask in my name. Until now you have not asked for anything in my name. Ask and you will receive, and your joy will be complete." In John 16:23–24, the Apostle Paul offered his wisdom on Christian giving while speaking to the Corinthians about spiritual gifts: "If I give all I possess to the poor and surrender my body to the flames, but have not love, I gain nothing."

Giving Life

Christians generally do not need to be reminded to give in the service of others. The question is how do we—you and I—best practice charity? My feeling is that we do it by expressing real love for our fellow human beings in whatever ways mean the most to those in need. Simply listening to the lonely or spending time with the bedridden can be an act of charity of great significance. You don't have to shower money and gifts on the needy—in fact, that may be the worst thing you could do. It is important to understand what needs are out there and how they can best be served. In fact, giving time, attention, and love may be of more lasting benefit than nearly any other gift.

There are as many ways to give as there are ways to suffer on this earth. The suffering of hurricane victims has inspired dramatic responses from Christian-spirited men and women. Yet there are other types of suffering that we good Christians need to address with our good deeds. Psalm 41:1–3 tells us:

> *Blessed is he who has regard for the weak; the LORD delivers him in times of trouble. The LORD will protect him and preserve his life; he will bless him in the land and not surrender him to the desire of his foes. The LORD will sustain him on his sickbed and restore him from his bed of illness.*

Sometimes my mother would hurt so much from lupus that she would cry out and it would break my heart. I'd tell her, "Don't cry, Mama. When I grow up you won't have to work or worry. I'll give you anything you want." As a child and as a teenager, I didn't fully realize that there was no cure I could buy for my mother's pains. God did allow her to live long enough for me to offer her much comfort before her death from this devastating disease that attacks black women in far greater numbers than those of other races.

It is estimated that lupus affects more than 1.5 million people in the United States. Sixty-four percent of all newly diagnosed cases in our country are black females. That is a striking statistic, but believe me, it is nothing like watching your mother in the throes of this terrible disease. Mine suffered for nearly twelve years before she was even diagnosed. It is a difficult disease to spot because the symptoms come and go. At times she appeared to be fine. But then, it would assert itself again. One day she would be functioning normally. The next she'd be in intensive care with swelling and soreness that rendered her barely able to draw breath.

I watched my mother suffer and vowed that I would do whatever I could to ease the suffering of others like her. God blessed me with wonderful family support as a child, and I've been blessed as an adult in many ways. In Luke 12:48 we are told: "From everyone who has been given much, much will be demanded; and from the one who has been entrusted with much, much more will be asked." God holds us accountable for the blessings we have received. If we've been showered with them, we must respond in kind. With that in mind, I've practiced philanthropy on many levels, but my most public effort is the organization my wife and I created to fight the diseases that have attacked our own family and others we've known and loved. Our organization is the Walt and Sonya Love Lupus and Cancer Research Foundation, which is a 501(c)(3) nonprofit organization. It's not a major charity like St. Jude's, but it is growing and it is doing some good and helping to ease suffering.

After surviving kidney cancer by the grace and mercy of God, and after watching my mother and others suffer from lupus, Sonya and I wanted to do what we could to encourage finding cures for cancer and lupus. Sonya also has several family members who've passed away from bouts with cancer and lupus. We created this foundation to show that we are willing to walk the talk as God's children. I believe it is our duty to practice charity in meaningful ways that positively impact the lives of others. This charity has deep meaning for us as well as for those it reaches out to, and it has thrived while God's own soundtrack played.

Gospel Grace

During my own bout with serious illness, there were two gospel songs that really ministered to my spirit. One was the John P. Kee and the New Life Community Choir song, "Jesus, He's

My King"; the second song was "Miracle Worker" recorded by gospel icon Rance Allen. In "Miracle Worker," Rance sings: "I looked in the mirror and what did I see? Another one of God's children looking back at me. He's miracle worker." We are all God's children, of course, and that means we must live his legacy of faith, hope, and charity. Sometimes we too can create miracles simply by giving of our talents and time for the benefit of others.

Gospel music glorifies God and thanks him for his love and the gift of faith. When I hear gospel artists sing his praises it evokes joy and excitement like nothing else can. Their music connects my spirit to God. Faith and love for God are as much a part of gospel music as sunshine is to California. God must be a gospel lover. I know I am. When I was a kid back in Creighton, our pastor and the deacons of the church sometimes arranged for gospel singing groups to come out to our little church. Often they'd performed in Pittsburgh and wanted to pick up on some extra gas money by singing for us. Our church was really small, but somehow they would get money together for groups like the Swan Silvertones and the Five Blind Boys. We didn't have a sound system, so these were more like jam sessions in your living room. It was God's music, sweet and pure! It also brought a touch of showbiz glitter to our little town because the performers would wear their stage outfits—bright suits and alligator shoes—and often they'd show up in a line of Cadillacs. Most of the people in our little community didn't have cars, so Cadillacs were like starships parked on our drab streets.

When I became a broadcaster, I always looked for opportunities to sneak a gospel tune or two onto the air, even with my rhythm and blues shows. I figured a little of God's music might do us all a little good. When we started *Gospel Traxx* in 1995 it was a true labor of love. My wife Sonya was the true authority on gospel in our family. She has a wealth of knowledge of the music, its history, and the performers. I got into it because it moved me and it took me back to my boyhood. Gospel music puts you in touch with your emotions, and I truly believe it brings you closer to God. I find it impossible to feel depressed or lethargic with gospel music playing. The Holy Spirit rides the melody and lifts you up.

Of course, my love of gospel is also rooted in the fact that this is true "soul" music. Gospel is a part of my African American heritage just as polkas are a part of Polish culture. When African slaves were brought to North America in chains, they brought with them their tribal music in the form of drumbeats, hand claps, and chants. Their native music evolved into field chants, songs, and hymns. In the 1930s, the son of a Baptist preacher and his church organist became known as the father of gospel music. Thomas Dorsey, a black man nicknamed "Georgia Tom," brought African-based roots music into the mass market by matching blues to religious themes. Dorsey performed with blues and jazz artists like Ma Rainey and her Wild Cats Jazz Band while also composing more than four hundred songs. His most famous was "Take My Hand, Precious Lord," written after his wife and son died in childbirth. So you know that his gospel came from the heart.

Today, gospel music outsells jazz and classical. Most black musicians, singers, writers, and producers are quick to tell you that their love of music is rooted in the gospel songs they learned in church as children. Many of them have told me this themselves. R&B and hip-hop artists like Usher are proud to say they started singing in church. In his case, Usher first performed in his grandfather's church in Knoxville, Tennessee. The Isley Brothers sang gospel before their R&B success. Others include Charlie Wilson of the Gap Band and Kenny "Babyface" Edmonds, who sang in the gospel choir in his hometown of Indianapolis. Brian McKnight is another former gospel singer, and several of his relatives are in the gospel group Take 6. And most of the great female pop and soul stars first learned their chops in the church choir loft—from Aretha Franklin, the daughter of famed Detroit preacher the Reverend C. L. Franklin, to Whitney and Cissy Houston, and Kelly Price and Michelle Williams of Destiny's Child.

The black church has produced more talented singers than any music school in the country. God has blessed these performers, and most freely acknowledge their debt to gospel music.

Tapping Talent

After making the decision to put our faith and love and Christian charity into action by starting the foundation, it seemed logical to enlist the help and services of people I work with in the music and broadcasting industry. I contacted many top gospel music artists, their managers, and their record label representatives and asked if they were willing to donate performances at fund-raisers for our foundation. Many artists have stepped up so far to help us get started. We've kept it small as we learn how to best approach these concerts. We've had crowds of 1,500 or so at our first efforts over the first two years. We have been blessed over the years to have many great gospel music performers help with our efforts to find a cure for lupus and cancer. I've had a wonderful core group who've told me time and again, "If you need us. We'll be there even if we have to change our schedules." God has given me favor to have so many wonderful people on my side. Those from the gospel music business are among the most talented and creative folks to toil in God's own vineyard.

My core group of people have included my personal musician—who is almost as important as my personal physician—Moses Tyson Jr. on the Hammond B3 organ; Christopher Lewis, who's a talented writer, producer, and artist; Darlene McCoy, who writes and sings; and a Christian comedian named Akintunde from Columbia, South Carolina. These other artists I really want you to take note of because they've always been there for us to answer the call, and we owe them our gratitude because we know it is easy to make promises but much more difficult to fulfill them. The Williams Brothers—who have two family members battling lupus—have performed with us on two occasions: in St. Louis and Kansas City, Missouri. Our host church in Kansas City was Christ Temple Church where Bishop Mark Tolbert is the pastor. He and his wife Emmelda, who fought off cancer six years ago, have become our biggest supporters, and they have offered to hold fund-raisers at their church for four years straight. Christ Temple also supports a Wellness Ministry.

Other gospel artists who've been with us include Byron Cage, Smokie Norful, the Mighty Clouds of Joy, Dottie Peoples, Dr. Charles G. Hayes and the Warriors, Evelyn Turrentine-Agee, Tri-I-Tee 5:7, Tonex, Luther Barnes and the Sunset

Jubilaires, Dorinda Clark-Cole, Kierra "KiKi" Sheard, Twinkie Clark, Norman Hutchins, Chester D.T. Baldwin, J Moss, Derrick Starks, Detrick Haddon, Rance Allen and the Rance Allen Group, Keith "Wonderboy" Johnson, the Sounds of Blackness, Rizen, Parkes Stewart, Marvin Sapp and Kurt Carr and the Kurt Carr Singers, Helen Baylor, Damon Little with Nu Beginnings, and Ramiyah. Oh, let's not forget the girl group Virtue.

These artists have inspired me with their encouraging words both on stage and off. Several of them have family members who have suffered with cancer or lupus. Several have lost loved ones to these diseases, and those loved ones have gone home with the Lord. These artists have not only shared their talents with our audiences who've come out to support our fundraisers. They've also shared their heartfelt words and emotions. And for that, I will forever be grateful to each and every one of them. I know they have other demands on their time. And I am grateful for their generosity. I also thank the record executives and artist managers who've supported our efforts by encouraging their artists to lend their support and making it possible for them to participate.

Generous Talent

There are many stories I could tell you about our "Love Crusade" fund-raisers that would make you laugh, cry, and or shake your head. Two years ago, we were going to Kansas City for a benefit and we needed a well-known "headliner" for the show. We contacted several artists, but none were available. I prayed about it and asked God, "What should I do, Lord?" He then put it in my spirit to call a young talented writer, producer, and artist who appeared on my R&B show *The Countdown.* Every now and then I decide to play some gospel music for my secular audience because I like to give people not just what they want, but what they need too. With a radio show targeted to an "urban" audience—which is an industry term used for blacks and Latinos—I really feel the need to sprinkle in heaping helpings of the "what they need" for my listeners.

When we started our *Gospel Traxx* radio program I needed jingles so I hired a rapper named Kirk Franklin. But before he could finish my jingles his record took off and so did he. His label sent a replacement, the talented Kurt Carr. He did a terrific job writing, producing, and singing the jingles, so I asked him to perform as the headliner at our Kansas City fund-raiser. I went to Kurt and I got straight answers from him. He looked at his calendar and told me he was going to be in Washington, DC, the night before but on that Sunday afternoon he could do our date if they could hook up the flights from DC to Kansas City.

But his record company at the time didn't share his generous spirit. For budgetary reasons, they refused to take care of the airfare for him, his musicians, and his singers. Nor would they pay for their hotels. So Sonya and I personally took care of his hotel rooms and Kurt, bless him, paid for all the plane tickets himself. Kurt was an angel and we thank God for his kindness and the love of Christ in his heart to help us at that event. He even hung around and signed autographs when they finished. To God be the glory!

Performers have many demands on their time, and they have to make a living, so we understand that it is often a sacrifice for them too. We honor their participation by not charging for tickets to their free performances. Instead, we ask for "love offer-ings" from those who attend. They can give any amount they want, whatever they feel is appropriate. Hopefully, people will appreciate that the concert is a benefit and contribute even be-yond what they would normally pay to see top artists. It doesn't always work out that way, but we've found that there are far more givers than takers out there. We have been blessed by their generosity and so have those who benefit from our foundation.

Spirit of Giving

Those who come to our fund-raisers have warmed our hearts. They are true Christians who love the Lord and they love God's people. Many have loved ones who've passed away from complications of lupus or have died of cancer. Some folks have had their own bouts with either lupus or cancer. They have asked us to pray for them too. We've also benefited from the charity of medical professionals who have supported our foun-dation. They see the need on a daily basis and they give not only of their talents, but their time and money too.

Whatever money is raised by our foundation is given away at the end of year to one cutting-edge cancer researcher and one cutting-edge lupus researcher. Several different organiza-tions over the last few years have given us names of researchers and the names of their organizations and what they're working on in their chosen fields. We read all the info, ask some ques-tions, and then try and make an informed decision with help from those who know and then give the money away. We've sent funds to both the UCLA's Jonsson Comprehensive Cancer Center Foundation in Los Angeles and the Lupus Center of

Excellence at Magee-Womens Hospital. The second is especially close to home, my childhood home, and the home of my heart. Magee is part of the University of Pittsburgh Medical Center. The Lupus Center is known for its world-class care. It is the only place in the country that offers a "one-stop shop" for all of the needs of lupus patients. My wife and I are hopeful that we will be able to do even more to help the wonderful medical professionals there seek a cure for those suffering from this dreadful affliction.

The Kingdom of God

In Mark 4:30–32, we are given the Parable of the Mustard Seed:

> *"What shall we say the kingdom of God is like, or what parable shall we use to describe it? It is like a mustard seed, which is the smallest seed you plant in the ground. Yet when planted, it grows and becomes the largest of all garden plants, with such big branches that the birds of the air can perch in its shade."*

Throughout this book I've emphasized that as Christians, we must put our faith into action so that we can continue to grow in Christ. It is a lifelong journey and as our faith and knowledge grow, new mysteries are revealed within the Bible. The more you know, the more you grow in faith—and the more opportunities open for you to practice the teachings of Jesus. God wants us to take care of the poor and needy in our society and when we do that we are blessed for being obedient to his wishes.

God loves us and he wants us to love those who are less fortunate in our midst. Jesus offers his testimony to this in John 14:12: "I tell you the truth, anyone who has faith in me will do what I have been doing." We have to put our faith in Jesus, and his Holy Spirit will give us the power of God to take the gospel around the world. That, in turn, will allow us to apply the love of Christ in feeding the poor, helping the poor, loving the poor, clothing the poor, housing the poor, caring for the poor, healing the sick, and teaching those who don't know about God what they should know about his love.

Heavenly Healing

In my testimony about my battle with kidney cancer I noted that at first I let Satan get the best of me. But I quickly remembered Jesus' teaching about having the faith of a mustard seed. I reached out to God through prayer and my prayers were answered. We must have faith if we expect to achieve our ordained destinies. Open your heart to God and he will guide you.

When Jesus talked about the "faith of a mustard seed" it was during the healing of a boy possessed by a demon. The boy's father asked Jesus to help heal the tormented boy "if you can do anything."

Jesus replies, "If you can? Everything is possible for him who believes." He then commanded the evil spirit to leave the boy and he was healed.

The lesson for us is that our faith in God must be maintained, even if it is just a tiny grain of belief. The mustard seed is very small, but when planted, watered, and nurtured, it grows into a large tree that glorifies God!

Let us all glorify God as his Christian soldiers on earth. When things get challenging and the evil spirit stands at your door, have faith. Call out in prayer to your Lord God Heavenly Father: Never give up, never give in, and never give out! Be strong and courageous because God is with you! Hallelujah! Hallelujah! Hallelujah!!

"For I know the plans I have for you," declares the LORD,
"plans to prosper you and not to harm you, plans to give you
hope and a future."

—JEREMIAH 29:11

ACKNOWLEDGMENTS

God has been good to me by putting strong, courageous, faithful, and intelligent believers in my life. Most of the individuals in my mother's family are at home with the Lord, but my mother has two brothers, Daniel and Leonard Hawkins. Uncle Dan and Uncle Len have been solid and caring male role models. Words can't express my love and admiration for them. Aunt Jean is now the matriarch of our small family back home in Pennsylvania. I love and respect her dearly. When I need earthly encouragement, I call Aunt Jean. My brother Dale, like me, is a living testimony to God's love and power. God brought you out and we thank him. My life, like most in society, is one continuous challenge. I want to thank my immediate family; my wife, Sonya, and son, Stephan, for all you do. The two of you inspired me to do this book.

I thank God for my editor Nancy Hancock at Simon & Schuster. She believed in what God was doing in me and through me. It's a blessing to work with and for you. Your team is awesome. Special thanks to my broadcasting agent Eric Weiss, who has always believed in my talents and ideas. My heartfelt thanks go to everyone at Dupree Miller Literary Agency and especially to Jan Miller, who walked me to the door that God opened, just as I told her it would. I can't write this without getting my shout on! Michael Broussard, formerly of Dupree Miller, moved on before we completed the book, but thanks to him for all of his efforts too. And to Nena Madonia, also of Dupree Miller, you are the best! Thanks for dotting all the i's and crossing all the t's. It truly was a pleasure working with you.

As I continue this journey I can't help but be mindful of all those in ministry who've been kind and encouraging to me as a newcomer. Bishop Mark C. Tolbert, Pastor of Christ Temple Church in Kansas City, MO; Bishop G. E. Patterson, Temple of Deliverance Church of God in Christ in Memphis, TN; Bishop Paul Morton, Pastor of Greater St. Stephens Full Gospel Church in New Orleans; Pastor Dante Rome of Bethel A.M.E. Church, Marysville, CA; Pastor Hurley C. Coleman Jr. of Coleman Temple in Saginaw, MI; Pastor Curtis Johnson of Valley Brook Outreach Baptist Church in Pelzer, SC.

Thanks also to Reverend Cecil "Chip" Murray, my pastor at First A.M.E. Church Los Angeles. It was a privilege to serve under your leadership for seven years. My appreciation goes out also to my current pastor, Rev. Dr. John J. Hunter at First A.M.E. in Los Angeles. Thanks for the opportunity to serve under your anointed leadership for the past two years. Thank you also, Pastor John, for permission to shoot our book cover at FAME. Love to my entire (FAME) family, especially to the Unity Choir members who posed for our book cover and Director Michael Curls. I am grateful also to photographer Julie Dennis-Thomas and her staff for an excellent photo shoot, which was really a lot of fun.

I thank Richard "Dick" Oppenheimer, my lifelong mentor and friend in the broadcasting industry, for all his guidance and continued encouragement. Mr. O, thanks for the first full-time job at KYOK, Houston. It began fulfilling God's destiny for my life.

I'd like to express my gratitude to Rick Roberts, who helped me learn the broadcasting fundamentals and to my ultimate mentor as a talent and broadcaster, Paul Drew. You and your wife, Ann, have been a true blessing. God gave me favor with both of you, which was part of his divine plan. Thank you.

Finally, I would like to acknowledge my co-writer for this book, Wes Smith. You came highly recommended and now I really know why! Your professionalism is outstanding. Your guidance was invaluable, and I can't thank you enough for helping me to find my voice and to express my innermost thoughts. Let's get ready for the next blockbuster.

ABOUT THE AUTHOR

For more than three decades, pioneering broadcaster Walt "Baby" Love has touched the lives of more than ten million listeners across the world with his award-winning radio programs *The Countdown with Walt Baby Love*, *The Urban AC Countdown*, *Gospel Traxx*, and *African Americans Making It Happen*.

Walt also served as the urban editor at *Radio and Records* newspaper for more than twenty years.

An ordained minister, Walt holds a master's degree from Fuller Theological Seminary and serves as an associate minister at First AME Church of Los Angeles. He and his wife, Sonya, are cofounders of the nonprofit Walt & Sonya Love Foundation for Cancer and Lupus Research in Los Angeles, where they live with their son, Stephan.